WHEN I AM
AN OLD WOMAN
I SHALL WEAR
PURPLE

WHEN I AM AN OLD WOMAN I SHALL WEAR PURPLE

An Anthology of Short Stories and Poetry

Papier-Maché Press
Manhattan Beach, CA

Papier-Maché Press
795 Via Manzana
Watsonville, California 95076 - (408) 726-2933

First Edition, Fourth Printing, December 1988

ISBN: 0-918949-02-5
Library of Congress Catalog Number: 87-042797

Editor: Sandra Martz
Cover Art: Deidre Scherer, "Laughing Rose," fabric and thread, Copyright ©1985, from the collection of Mr. and Mrs. Stanley Feldberg.
Design and typography: Lane Relyea
Editorial Assistance: Lee Rathbone and Roberta Shepherd
Copyediting: Bobbie Goodwin

Grateful acknowledgement for permission to reprint is made as follows: *Appalachian Heritage* for "Near Places, Far Places" by Sarah Barnhill; *Footwork* for "Aunt Marie at 99" by Tom Benediktsson; *Lion Tamer* (Waterford Press, ©1987 by Lillian Morrison) for "The Thugs" by Mura Dehn; *Kalliope, Dekalb Literary Journal,* and *Waiting for Order* for "Come to Me" by Sue Saniel Elkind; *Odessa Poetry Review* for "Late Autumn Woods" by Rina Ferrarelli; *New Mexico Quarterly* for "To an Old Woman" ©1986 by Rafael Jesús González; *Day Tonight Night Today #16* for "The Pianist" by Carolyn J. Fairweather Hughes; *Friendly Women* for "Becoming Sixty" by Ruth Harriet Jacobs and *Button, Button, Who Has the Button* for "Bag Ladies" ©1983 by Ruth Harriet Jacobs; *The Red Bluff, CA, Daily News* for "Investment of Worth" by Terri Jewell; *Rose in the Afternoon* (J.M. Dent and Sons) for "Warning" by Jenny Joseph; *Fiction West* for "The Changes" ©1981 by Fionna Perkins; *The Problem with Eden* (Armstrong State College Press) for "Clearing the Path" ©1985 by Elisavietta Ritchie; *Artemis* for "Dear Paul Newman" by Marie Kennedy Robins; *Ellipsis* for "Sitty Victoria" by Vicki Salloum; *Morning of the Red-Tailed Hawk* (Green River Press) for "A Letter from Elvira" ©1981 by Bettie Sellers; *Full Moon* for "Last Visit to Grandmother" by Enid Shomer; *Ask the Dreamer Where Night Begins* for "Post Humus" by Patti Tana, ©1986 Kendall/Hunt Publishing Company; *Loonfeather* for "Oh, That Shoestore Used to Be Mine" ©1986 by Randeane Doolittle Tetu. Additional copyrights: "Like Mother, Like Daughter" ©1986 by Susan S. Jacobson and "Two Willow Chairs" ©1985 by Jess Wells.

To my Grandmother, Mildred Anna Archer, who gave me hope, and to my Mother, Lula Jo Gregory, who gave me wisdom.

-Sandra Martz, Editor

Contents

Warning

Jenny Joseph

When I am an old woman I shall wear purple
With a red hat which doesn't go, and doesn't suit me.
And I shall spend my pension on brandy and summer gloves
And satin sandals, and say we've no money for butter.
I shall sit down on the pavement when I'm tired
And gobble up samples in shops and press alarm bells
And run my stick along the public railings
And make up for the sobriety of my youth.
I shall go out in my slippers in the rain
And pick the flowers in other people's gardens
And learn to spit.

You can wear terrible shirts and grow more fat
And eat three pounds of sausages at a go
Or only bread and pickle for a week
And hoard pens and pencils and beermats and things in boxes.

But now we must have clothes that keep us dry
And pay our rent and not swear in the street
And set a good example for the children.
We must have friends to dinner and read the papers.

But maybe I ought to practise a little now?
So people who know me are not too shocked and surprised
When suddenly I am old, and start to wear purple.

Lyn Cowan, Ruby at the Fair

Sitty Victoria
Vicki Salloum

"Aunt Alma," I asked yesterday, "why you sticking Sitty in the 'tomb'?"

She got angry. "It ain't the 'tomb'. It's The Asylum For The Aged."

"Then why you sticking Sitty in The Asylum For The Aged?"

"Victoria, I'm over eighty. I can't care for her no more. And what with you gone..."

I could see Aunt Alma crying and I really got scared because I knew then she was serious. "I'm not going!" I said. "I'm staying here with her! I can stay and care for her!"

"Young lady!" she said. "You got to get an education. That's what Mama always wanted, what Papa would have wanted. You just go and pack your things. You'll miss that plane tomorrow morning."

I put my hands down on my hips.

"Aunt Alma," I said, "the woman raised eleven kids, raised you and Uncle Youssef, raised me all those years after Mama and Daddy died and now she has nobody else you want to stick her in the 'tomb'?

"Aunt Alma," I said, "what the hell's wrong with you ?"

And then she slapped me in the face and I didn't know what else to do so I went and sat with Sitty.

It's light. I sneak a peek from Sitty's bedroom door. She rises from the bed, bracing herself with blotched and shriveled arms. She sits in a giltwood armchair putting on her stockings, guiding an elastic garter up her swollen leg.

I walk through the back porch into the kitchen. Over the sink, through the open window, I see the morning come. A strange September morning. A loon in the air. The sky has taken on an eerie glow. I put on a pot of coffee, crack some eggs. Beyond the kitchen window an unusual morning wind turns suddenly wild, hurling leaves across the Summervilles' patio and against the side of their garage.

"Sabah alkheir, Sitty Victoria."

I bring her eggs to the porch. Sitty's sitting on the green sofa where she always sits. *"Ana bahibbik,* darlin'. *Inshallah nimti mnih."* She's always teaching me Arabic words, things like *'Allah maik'* and *'Allah yakun'*—'God be with you,' 'God go with you.'

I catch the leg of a TV tray, slide it in front of her. I sit the breakfast tray down. Try to hand her an Arabic paper but she doesn't see me.

"Sitty," I'm on my knees, my face square in hers, "there's something I got to tell you, darlin'."

I touch her hand. It's cold. She's watching the wind bend the branches of a live oak next door. It's no use. I sit down, my arm touching hers, think about being stuck on that jet tomorrow. Think about a lot of things. How I've never been without her. How when I was a little girl, we'd pass the gardenia bushes by the Girl Scout hut at the Aurelia Street park where she'd take me swinging on clear April mornings and I could smell eternity. I swear I don't believe I'll ever see her again. She'll die in that place.

Uncle Youssef said her hair was raven black. Now it's white, streaked with yellow, pulled back in a bun at the nape of her neck. Aunt said she was tall, statuesque in her prime. We talked about it when I was pestering her once. We were chopping up parsley and tomatoes for *tabbouleh.*

"She left Beirut by herself, Victoria. Marry your Jiddy in the cathedral in New Orleans. They was peddlers over there half starving living over Mandot's Bakery on Chartres Street."

Aunt went to the cupboard, fetched a wooden bowl. "I was

sixteen when she told Papa we was moving here: 'Najeeb, we ain't gonna be peddling pans no more.'

"Sure 'nough, he loaded the wagon, put ten kids in it, with your Daddy, Victoria, still full in her stomach, and you'd a thought we was crossing a continent with how excited we all was at five in the morning heading for our new home on the Mississippi Coast."

Aunt slid the tomatoes in the bowl, started chopping more. Her hands never ceased. "I don't know how she done everything — got us the big house and that building on Pass Road that was our dry goods store. Papa tease her, call her a little immigrant girl with *kibbi nayyi* on her fingers and a brain bigger 'n his, bigger 'n most. After the jump, she built a town for him."

I look at her now, all hunched, shriveled, think how time always changes things. I raise my cup, sip lukewarm coffee and try to think how old she is. Aunt said 104; Uncle Youssef, 108. Nobody alive knows. I glance outside, feel the ruckus in the air, hear the sky belting out angry screams. Strips of old newspaper and hot dog wrappers go flying over the Summervilles' fence and into our yard, but Sitty only sits, her hands in her lap, her brow furrowed, her head bowed. *Ya haram,* poor thing. She never does a thing but sit out here.

Once she tried to plant pecan trees way in the back near old lady Miller's but Aunt pitched a fit and brought her back inside. That's the next to last time she ever left this house. The last was when they caught her walking to the big house in that storm. She really missed the big house. Mayor Falk was cruising the beachfront highway when he saw her. He put her in his car and lectured her proper and deposited her safely at Aunt Alma's door. Now she won't do a thing but sit out here and think old thoughts, relive old memories. I wonder if she's thinking about what Jiddy did?

Aunt told me about it. She said, " Trouble has a way of sneaking up on you. It come for Mama at closing time." Sitty was closing out the register when the deputies came. Old Sheriff Elmo Cobb's deputies. They took her up to the dingy roof of the Elnora Hotel. Took Daddy and Aunt Alma and Uncle Youssef up, too.

"But why, Aunt Alma? Why'd y'all all go up there?"

"Cuz," she said, "that's where Papa was. Victoria, I'm trying to tell you. Your Granddaddy—your Jiddy—he done killed himself."

Aunt Alma said she'd never forget that night—it was 1928 or '29 or something—or forget her Papa falling those fifteen stories from the dingy roof of the Elnora. Or forget her Mama standing there, her eyes all over him, as was the whole Pass Christian High basketball crowd that jammed Morey's Ice Cream Parlor across the street from the Elnora following the biggest game of the season, the game Pass Christian won against Biloxi High, whopped the socks off them in their first time playing each other since five years before when they had that big free-for-all in the Biloxi gym. And all eyes on her Papa, stunned and terrible, but none so terrible as her Mama's eyes.

"Why, Aunt Alma? Why'd Jiddy kill himself? Eleven kids, a dry goods store, a woman fine as Sitty. Why'd he want to die for?"

"Papa borrowed a lot of money to put in the stock market."

She said Sitty tried her best to talk Jiddy down, said she never gave up on him, never stopped talking to him in that voice of hers that makes you believe you can do anything, going on about how the children needed him, with all the need stuck in her eyes, and how important a man he was to her and how she'd always believed in him, after thirty-three years never would stop believing in him, how he wasn't to blame for what was done, he was only trying to help the family out. "We love you for that, my darling Najeeb, love you for what you tried to do for us; we're in God's hands now, Najeeb; God will see us through all this; God will take care

of us, now, Najeeb; please come home with me now, Najeeb; oh please, dear God, come home with me..." And, afterwards, Sheriff Cobb's deputies had to take them home.

I collect the breakfast tray, bring it to the kitchen. It's still early morning but the sky is turning dark. I dump cold grits in the garbage pail, think about the thousand things I got to do before I leave. Through the open window, the wind's howling. Aunt's old teapot's in pieces in the sink. I go to the hall closet, take down the transistor radio. Early storm warnings are saying a hurricane's headed our way. I phone Aunt Alma, who's off visiting cousin Flora, then Uncle Youssef in case he doesn't know. He says he's come back from taking his lugger "The Jezebel" from the Gulf of Mexico harbor to the Back Bay of Biloxi. He says I should get moving, too, board the windows with plywood, fill the tub with water, help out around here.

But I go back to the porch and settle down beside her, recall Aunt Alma's words on the only day she ever felt like talking about the subject. She said, "Mama never took the easy way out." She said after that terrible night, Sitty worked like a dog paying back Jiddy's creditors, though the menfolk advised her not to do that, to file for bankruptcy instead, because how could she expect to run that store and raise eleven kids and pay his debts all in a depression. But Aunt said Sitty never paid those men a mind. "Bankruptcy's a disgrace," she told those men, "and I'll never disgrace Najeeb's good name."

I look at her now, see how fragile she is, so worn and decrepit you'd think her flesh would dry up and crumble to the floor so there'd be nothing left but piles of flesh and bone to take a broom to. I take her hand; what does it matter anymore. Jiddy's gone. Mansour, her eldest, died right after him. Daddy, the one she loved so much, gone. Naome and Fayad, killed with their friends playing chicken with a freight train. And all the rest of them taken by sickness, except Aunt and Uncle Youssef.

Lori Burkhalter, Rose

I hold up my palm. Flit it past her face, feel the grief like a thousand needles.

"Sitty, darlin'," I can't stand it any longer. "I'm leaving for St. Mary's College on Monday."

I listen for a sound, some encouragement to go on, then steel myself against this onslaught of silence.

"And...darlin'..." I say, "Aunt can't keep you anymore. She's found a nice...home...for you..."

Her muzzy gaze settles on a spot somewhere in her lap.

"I'm going to write you every day. I promise I will..."

I need to say something more, reassure somebody, her or myself. I feel this panic coming on like I did before the accident, Mama and Daddy's accident, when I was so torn up inside and nobody even told me something irreversible would happen. "Oh Sitty, I love you so, so much." But the words come out formal and ominous and sad.

We sit here together with nothing left. And then she looks at me. A sweetness fills her face. She cradles my cheeks in both her hands, kisses each twice in Arabic style. *"Ayni habibi,"* she says, "my eye and my love."

I am crying so hard and when I look at her again, she's staring at the kitchen. Her eyes are beautiful, a young woman's eyes. I know what's going on. She's back in the kitchen of the big house, fixing *sheik ik mihshee* and *hummus bi taheeni* with her girls in the days she ruled over that kitchen, making Sunday buffets and holiday feasts for when kin came to call.

That's where she belongs, in that high-ceilinged house. Not here. Now. There's no need of her now.

Only one thing I know: she can't rot in that tomb. Sitty and I, we'll move back to the big house. She and I lived there when Mama and Daddy were alive. And when they died—while turning in the front drive off the dark beach highway—she raised me alone there. Up till three years ago when Aunt Alma's husband,

Uncle Abdou, dropped dead and we moved in with her.

This house is okay, but there'll never be another house for us like the big house with its grounds as huge as a football field and giant oaks all around and marigolds and hollyhocks growing near the slave house she used for a washhouse. Sitty bought that house and raised eleven children in it and raised me in it.

Still, it'd never work out. The old roof leaks and the balcony of the big house is about to cave in and the attic fan's broken and the paint's peeled and chipped. *Ya haram,* poor thing. She can't take the stairs anymore. Besides, there're no more kids for her to go back to. Not Daddy anymore. Not Mansour, Naome, Fayad, Jemille, Fedwah, Isabelle, Sadie, Shafee. Not Mama, either. Or Jiddy. It's no good living in a house with all those memories.

I look away. Look into the fading light. Bits of charcoal from the barbecue pit go flying across the terrace and slam into a lamp-post. Those gale winds rage steady now. That screeching sends a chill up me, makes me know what God can do in a second. That's what Aunt said once, surveying the rubble after lightning struck the fence in front of the big house and sent it crashing down: she knew what God could do in a second. She knew His majesty. I can feel the wind's majesty as it slaps the branches of a live oak. Every bush, tree and shrub in Aunt's back yard is doing a fast jitterbug, whirling, swirling; boogieing to the beat. Sitty's eyes keep time. She sees the makings of anarchy out there.

"Let's go to the front parlor." I try to take her arm. She'll have none of it. She's luminous now, as though a blast of winter cold has sprayed her in the summer. This stormy song and dance is making her frisky. Her eyes are incandescent; she gives me such a look. Aunt locked herself out of the house one time on a visit to Sitty and me when we lived in the big house. She got that look, too, after the initial shock wore off and she wondered who she'd get to unlock the door for her, Uncle Abdou or Mama and Daddy, then remembered with horror there was no one left to unlock the door, not Abdou, anyway, Mama and Daddy, anyway, and the silliness crossed her mind about the time the horror did, that what was she getting so excited about when Uncle Abdou was dead, Mama and Daddy were dead, what was so important ever again for her to worry about, that same intoxicating feeling of having nothing left to lose is what's shining in Sitty's eyes, same as it was in Aunt's eyes.

I reach for her arm again. She's pliable this time, puts up no fuss as I help her to the couch. Once standing, she presses her fingers sternly against my cheek. Her eyes are stern, too, a worried mother's eyes. She needs no words for what she's saying: *Allah maik, Allah maik.* My heart nearly stops. There's a walker in the corner directly to her left. She makes her way with it to the back porch door. Five tortoise steps, she lifts the top latch. She turns the knob. Opens the door. Frowning, she glances at the steps below, braces for what's coming and proceeds ahead.

The screeching, angry winds slam against her scalp, unraveling her hair from its place in her bun. Delicately, deliberately as a surgeon's hands move, she places both her hands on the wrought-iron rail and lowers her body sideways down the steps. I want to run after her, drape a shawl around her, warm the soft, fleshy mass of her cold, frail arms. Instead, I watch as her dress whips at her thighs and her hair swirls like a young girl's again. Even in good weather she couldn't take these steps alone. Even in good weather she wouldn't leave her walker behind. Even in good weather she could not get far. Still, she continues on, as doughty and durable as I have ever seen, treating each step like a sleek-edged cliff, unswerving, unerring, meticulous in her movements, till she departs the bottom step and is safely to the ground. Her feet planted firmly on the red flagstone, she loosens her hold on the rail, pauses to collect herself and walks into the howling wind.

At one point she looks back. Her eyes are like a child's. When they meet mine, they recoil. The grief is in them for what they've seen. Don't worry about me, darlin'. I'll be fine, *Allah yakun,* Sitty. God go with you.

I run to catch up with her. Hand her the walker. She takes it from my hand and motions me away. With enormous composure, she walks across the terrace, past the wildly blowing azaleas in Aunt's back yard, trampling the newly-planted begonias, till she reaches the driveway at the side of the house. She trudges up the driveway bound for the front of the house, her head jutting forward, her body forging on through the wind and rain.

In time, I cannot see her. I walk back to the house. Go to the front parlor. Wait beside a window. The fierce, raging winds sound like sledgehammers against the walls, but I can hardly hear for my own heart pounding. At the window, I see the fifteen-foot tides of the Mississippi Sound make a memory of the man-made beach on their journey over the seawall and across the lower highway. Soon the upper highway will be a memory, too. And her? I see her trekking up the front drive. It's not hard to imagine what madness she's planned: heave a left at the sidewalk that adjoins Highway 90, follow it three blocks till it takes her to the big house, one final scurry through those high-ceilinged rooms, rouse the long-time sleeping, hear the sound of their young voices, see a face or two. Never mind this scruffy storm. What's all the fuss about. It's surely worth the dying, so long they've all been gone.

The gale winds attack her as she tries to reach the sidewalk, beat her with a frenzy and finally lay her down. I watch the walker go racing down the block past the Woodward home, hear the screams of the racing deathman after her. I long to go after her, hold her in my arms, keep her beside me always, love her forever. But I walk back to the porch like it's all a dream. Sit on the green sofa where she used to sit. Think how I'll be leaving this town.

Grandma Sits Down

Rick Kempa

Her knees lean against the front of the battered rocker,
getting their bearings, while she frowns out the window
at the garden, or squints into the poplars
to see if the sparrow-hawks have returned. Slowly,
flat-footedly, like a fashion doll in the department store,

she rotates, knees locked, keeping contact
with the chair. Her hands grope for, find, grip the knobs
at the ends of the wooden arms. She's not looking
at anything now, it hurts, she's concentrating.
Holding her breath like an astronaut, knuckles white

around the knobs, she lets herself fall.
The chair shudders, reels backwards, hangs
for a very long instant on the coasters' rims (her eyes
are shut, head pressed back) and then begins to oscillate.
She breathes out: Another successful maneuver, nothing

to be especially pleased about. She knows
not to take for granted she can get back up. Still,
the wind of her motion cools her cheeks. She continues
with the letter she's been writing: "The earth is beginning
to thaw. I am anxious to plant some seeds."

Aunt Marie at 99

Tom Benediktsson

You kept your hair bound tight all your life,
but now it falls over your fierce Apache nose.
"I just put in the time now," you say,

and your vague eyes lift serenely
past the roses I brought to where
cats lounge in the rest home window,

bring you an image of Mert Melugin
lounging in the dairy, talking to the cats,
fingers busy with a cigarette, August so hot

roses never had a chance, cats in the dairy
like melted butter — "But what's that worth?
Used to play pinochle but now I can't see to cheat!"

(and unspoken, "They all died, and bird-boned
old women are useless.") Smoke from August slash fires
blanks out the hills, and "Who's there?" you cry

with the startled anger that finally came
when you let your hair fall, too late
for anything but itself.

Here, Take My Words

Karen Brodine

I prefer to believe that the last time we saw each other, she rushed out of the house in a rage and hitchhiked home to her shack.

But this isn't fiction. So I have to say that the last time I say hello to that face, she looks past me to the wall and I'm not her granddaughter anymore, it can't matter to her anymore.

"Nabana," she says, "nabana!" and I peel one.

□

Her skin shines down the rest home hall like a beacon.

She is naked from the waist and her body gleams as if it is a wet, white seal. Her breasts are longer and heavier than I remember and seeming to fade, the nipples soft and undefined from the whole breast. She leans forward from the straps that bind her to the chair, shifting her weight back and forth. She says hello to my mother but doesn't seem to see me.

"I'm hungry, don't you have a little something?"

"Didn't they give you breakfast, mother?"

"I don't know, Mary. It isn't enough. Don't you have a little something?"

We have two bananas in the brown paper sack with two pairs of new socks—with blue stripes. The stripes make me mad, somehow, they are so cheerful.

"Get your clothes back on now, mother. Here's your robe. Let's put your clothes back on. Karen, find her other slipper—it's lost." We talk of her in the third person, as if she isn't there.

"Lost who? Who's lost?"

"Mother, we've lost your slipper. I've got to get your clothes together."

"Get me together. Then we can all be together fine," she snorts sarcastically.

Here it is under the bed. We put the fuzzy slipper on her hard claw foot, clenched and curved from no use.

☐

"Karen's here," my mother says.

"Where?"

"Right here," I say.

"You don't look like Karen."

"Maybe you're remembering me when I was little. And besides I'm wearing a hat."

"I don't recognize you."

"I recognized you right away, grandma."

"You did? That's good. How are you?"

"Oh, I'm fine."

"Well, I wish I was fine. Then we'd all be fine together."

She is picking at her buttons, trying to slip out of her robe. "Mother, don't take your clothes off again," says my mother.

"Why not?"

"Because you'll catch cold," I lie to her, feeling foolish. The room is very warm.

"Because they don't like it," my mother says, more honest.

We watch her hands roving like two determined animals over the robe. Her fingers light on a corner of it and she pulls it up. "Give me a look at this. What does it say?"

"Grandma, you can't read your robe and you can't eat your socks." She almost laughs at this. Then she looks hard at me, and points.

"Give me the little girl in there. Give me the little girl."

She changes the subject. "I'd like to get back to what I had."

"You had a lot."

"I did?" She brightens, thinking maybe of wished-for land, the ship to come in, the lucky break, the good job that leered around the corner.

"Yes. You had a lot. You're the strongest person I know."

"I'm glad to hear that," she says and her eyes focus on mine. We stare unsmiling at one another for a minute. I imagine that something goes between us, unspoken but solid, yet, I'm not sure. Maybe it's just that I *want* some signal from her.

"Get me out of here," she says, pulling at the straps.

"Where would you go then, if you could leave?"

"Oh, I'd be going toward home. Get me a phone."

"Grandma, I can't, but who would you call?"

"I'd call for something useful."

"Well, they'll bring you your lunch soon," says my mom. "That's useful."

"I don't want lunch. Then I'll be like a lake."

I take her socks out and print on them with a marker. H. Pierce in red letters. She watches curiously.

"Can you sign my socks?"

A nurse comes in to say hello. "Gee, Harriet, you're not talking much." The nurse turns to us. "Usually she just chatters and chatters — gee, Harriet, you're not saying much. See you later."

There's a long silence. Then my grandmother looks at me and extends her hand, palm up. "Here," she says, "take my words."

I realize she has been hurt by the woman's words. My mother says, "Oh, don't pay attention to that woman, darlin."

"Why?"

"Because, mother, it doesn't matter. It's all right."

It is time for us to leave because we can't bear to stay any longer. An hour seems like a long time. "Good-bye," she says, politely, formally, to me, and as we leave, she is slowly shedding her clothes like soft, wilting leaves.

The Trouble Was Meals

Elizabeth Bennett

Dad was the head of the family, for sure.
When he got us all together
it meant either a baby was on the way
or we were moving. So when the question was put,
How would it be if Grandma came to live with us?
I thought, no big deal.
I was glad we weren't moving.

I found a picture of Grandma,
a young dancer in a dress, sequins and feathers.
She had me tape it onto the mirror
over the dresser where she kept Grandpa's remains,
his gold cufflinks, glass eye.

It was all right,
Grandma the dancer in residence,
all right for me, hard for Mother.
Dad would come home, pour a glass of Old Crow Bourbon,
one for Mother, drink them both.

The trouble was meals.
Dad was used to holding forth
and the first night, halfway through Chicken Cacciatore
Grandma turned and said, "Rest your gums, dear."
She called everyone dear, all of us, the mailman,
even the exterminator.
She took to humming in a loud voice
and dropping her knife and fork on the floor.

One night she shouted, "Leftovers, leftovers,
where's the original?" and shoved her plate
on the floor. Baby threw his bottle
on top of the broken china. The plate crash
became a regular occurrence.

Fridays at school our teacher read us poetry,
"Poitry," she called it. One went,
"Old age is a flight of small cheeping birds…"*
I didn't like poetry. What I liked was Shop.
I made a wooden bowl, sanded the rim smooth,
carved my initials on the bottom.
I brought it home to Grandma
and we served her dinner in it every night.
She still shoved it on the floor
but nothing broke.

When I was at the orthodontist's one afternoon,
Grandma took a nap and never woke up.
We cleaned out her room. I helped Mother.
She was in a mood to throw everything out,
flannel sheets that smelled of urine, everything.
She only kept the picture. That night after dinner
I found the bowl in the trash.
Dad said, we won't need *that* anymore,
but I washed and dried it
and put it on the shelf next to Old Crow
so I could find it when Mother got old.

*"To Waken An Old Lady" by William Carlos Williams from *Collected Earlier Poems of William Carlos Williams,* New Directions Publishing Company.

Like Mother, Like Daughter

Susan S. Jacobson

"When are you coming?"
"On Sunday, why?"
"Because I want to get
some things, make the bed..."
"Oh, Mom," she said.
I felt an echo in me:
I had made the beds
just the week before
on a visit to my mother's,
because of her back.
Always before she had,
but now I did, knowing
where everything was:
I had moved her there.

Looking for recipes
of dishes my daughter likes,
I found the ones for meals
I had made my mother,
in her new kitchen,
and put them away
like an echo in a drawer.
Reviewing their ways,
looking for similarities
in their rhythms
(there were none);
I weighed them against
my need to be alone.

I am related to neither now
(their blue eyes are so dissimilar)
and yet I am their link.
There are echoes back
and forth through me:
I live alone, as do
my mother and my daughter,
none of us in the house
where we were raised or
spent our marriages.
Each of us is careful
of the others, unyielding
in small significant ways.

I now mother my mother
when I can no longer
mother my daughter
who is older than I
have ever felt myself to be.

Near Places, Far Places

Sarah Barnhill

We are both widows, Momma and me, and we live together under the same roof. When my husband died it seemed the right thing to do for me to move back home, so my boy Cleeve and me did, did move in with Momma, since she didn't have nobody and I didn't have nobody. Then Cleeve went and got hisself in trouble and had to leave home and now there's just Momma and me. Two women in a big old white house on the Asheville highway. We got a good view though, of the river and the valley and the mountains all around. And a good view is more than a lot of people got.

I was already living there with Momma when Mr. Van Fleet showed up. He came from Delray Beach, Florida, and drove up here every year to escape the heat. Sometimes his wife came with him, but she didn't like the mountains. She got carsick, and it rained too much to suit her. She was with him that year he stopped the first time though, and when she got out of the car, she stretched to get the kinks out and stood by the car door with her hands on her back. She had on dark glasses as big as beer mats, and she said nothing about the quilts.

Mr. Van Fleet had seen the quilts hanging on the clothesline, six of them stretched out in the sun to dry. We watched him stop in the middle of the highway, back his car up, and drive up to the house. He told us he was Mr. Van Fleet from Delray Beach, Florida, and offered to buy every last quilt.

Momma likes her quilts but Momma also likes making a dollar, so I wasn't too surprised when she agreed to sell all but one. She let him have Double Wedding Ring, Drunkard's Path, Goose in the Pond, and Steps to the Altar and Rob Peter, Pay Paul. But when it come to Widow's Mite she put on the brakes.

Photo by Rod Bradley

"It's got bullion stitching in it," she said. "And a piece from my momma's wedding dress."

"But you know there's pieces of Grannie's wedding dress in nearly every quilt you got," I told her.

"I know. But this one's different. Each of them gold coins stitched into every square's different. Just look at that work. And see here," she poked the quilt up at me, "this one's got Momma's initials stitched into it."

And there it was — ARC, for Addie Rae Case, stitched into the little yellow circle made out to look like a coin that was supposed to be part of the widow's mite.

"He'd give you a good price for it."

"I know. But this one's different."

"You are a stubborn soul, Momma."

"I know that too," she said.

Mr. Van Fleet came back the next summer and the summer after that and bought more quilts. French Bouquet and Burgoyne's Quilt and Noonday Lily. Others too, but I can't remember them all. And every summer he asked Momma would she part with Widow's Mite and every summer Momma said no.

Last August we were sitting on the porch shucking corn, working our way through half a dozen ears Moon had brought in early that morning before me or her was out of bed. Moon is my oldest boy and him and another man worked sixteen acres of bottom land near the International plant they'd been renting for the last seven years. This was the last summer for the corn though, and for everything — the tobacco and the beans and the tomatoes. International bought the land for a new extension and a parking lot, and as soon as Moon harvested the last ear of corn they started to break ground.

The phone rang. I had so much corn silk stuck all over me that Momma went to get it. She was gone a long time for her since she doesn't like talking on the phone, and when she came back she said it was Mr. Van Fleet and that he was heading back to Florida day after tomorrow.

"That's early," I said. "He usually stays till after the leaves turn."

"He says his wife wants him to get home."

"Something's not right here. When the man likes quilts and the wife tells him to get hisself home," I said. "But I reckon that's Florida for you."

"He's still going on about Widow's Mite. He offered me three hundred and fifty dollars for it this time."

"Take it," I said. "When Moon loses this land we're all going to need every little bit we can get."

"What's anybody need a quilt in Delray Beach, Florida, for anyway?"

"This corn is full of cut worms. Moon says rain early in the summer brings them on." This green worm stuck its head up at me and waved back and forth like someone's finger coaxing me on—to trouble, no doubt. I flicked it down onto the newspaper where all the shucks and silks was piled up.

"You reckon he's making something for hisself out of this?" Momma said.

"He's lucky to clear a dollar a bushel."

"Not Moon. Mr. Van Fleet."

I sat there looking down at the rows of pyramids we'd stacked the corn into. Most of the ears we froze just as they were. Some of it I made into creamed corn and filled enough quart bags for Moon and his family when they came for Sunday dinner. The rest I just put into little pint bags for me and Momma. I sat there looking down at those ears of corn wondering what to say about Mr. Van Fleet from Delray Beach, Florida.

Finally I said, "He doesn't need money, Momma. He's got two houses we know of, and you seen his car and his clothes."

I didn't tell Momma, but the thing I liked best—the only thing

I reckon—about Mr. Van Fleet was looking at him. I don't mean he was handsome, because he weren't. He was bald on top and had a thin face and wore funny little glasses that pinched his nose. But he was about the cleanest man I have ever seen and his clothes always looked like he'd just got them out the dry cleaners. Sometimes he wore a gold chain around his neck, and once he had on a shiny blue, zip-up boiler suit. But he didn't look like a mechanic. He looked like an astronaut. Moon and Cleeve are the best boys in the world, even if Cleeve did get in trouble and get sent down to Raleigh, but I know that they'll never look like Mr. Van Fleet. It isn't in their nature.

"He collects them, Momma. Just like Moon and Cleeve collected all those license plates they tacked up inside the shed. He's retired and he's got money and he likes to collect things. And," I stopped and looked straight at Momma because I wanted her to take this last point in, "he wants Widow's Mite bad enough to give you three hundred and fifty dollars for it."

Momma set her jaw the way she does when something doesn't please her, and she looked out across the valley, past the sourwoods that were beginning to turn red and their feathery blossoms that hung down like peacock tails, past the smoke stacks of the International plant, past the old quarry cut at Bledsoe, and on to the mountains that circle the whole valley.

"Esther," she finally said to me, "you and me are both old women. A person would think you'd know by now that there's some things you don't never get back once you let them get away."

"Don't talk mopey, Momma."

"This ain't mopey. This is facts."

No use saying any more when Momma was like this, so we picked up the corn mess and went inside to start supper.

That evening we were setting on the porch when I saw his car between the gaps in the althea hedge that lines the driveway up to the house. It was creeping along, trying not to hit the ruts and potholes we hadn't gotten around to fixing since all the rain in July. Blue car, althea, blue car, althea, it went.

"You didn't tell me he was coming," I said to Momma.

"He said he might. I didn't say not to."

That gave me hope. Maybe she'd changed her mind about Widow's Mite.

Whenever Mr. Van Fleet came to visit he put me in a strange way. From everything he said I figured he was four or five years younger than me, but he always made me feel like I was younger, and not in the good sense that old women like to feel younger. It was more like him and Momma was the grown-ups and I was just the little kid who didn't know nothing. So when he came I usually just sat on my hands and didn't say much. They mostly talked about quilts anyway.

I watched him get out the car and thought he looked like something from TV. He had on white tennis shoes and white socks with a word stitched into the top that I couldn't see so clear. In fact, he had writing on everything, on his shirt and his short pants that had big deep pockets in them. I had never seen his bare legs before and I hadn't expected them to have such muscles in them. He was trim, I'll have to admit, no rolls on his waist like even Moon and Cleeve have. Brown, too, brown like all those folks from Florida. Like burnt biscuits, Momma said once.

"So how's tricks?" he said as he came up the porch steps. He was always saying things like that — "How's tricks?" and "Hang in there" and "Have a good one." I don't care for such talk, personally.

But Momma seemed to pay no attention, just got up from her chair and said, "Evening."

Momma told me to get some tomato juice I had just made and when everybody got all settled down, talk turned to what it always turned to: quilts.

"I tell you, Molly, this morning in that shop in Biltmore

Forest I saw in their window a Widow's Mite for three hundred dollars. God's truth. That's why I upped my offer to three fifty."

"Whyn't you go ahead and buy that one?" Momma said.

"No antique value. And the filler was cheap. Probably just an old blanket." He drank some of his tomato juice but you could tell he paid no attention to what he was drinking. "And — this is the clincher — the blocks were quilted separately. The piecing gave it all away."

Momma said, "That's like plucking a chicken after it's baked."

They kept up such talk for a good thirty minutes while I just sat there and watched the dusk come in.

After a while, I began to think about all those quilts Mr. Van Fleet had bought. Wondering where Steps to the Altar and Drunkard's Path were, if they lay folded over a bed in a bright white bedroom that looked out over the blue ocean, or if Rob Peter, Pay Paul was draped over one of those rope hammocks you could lay down in and see palm trees and flowers that bloom the whole year long. It wasn't that I missed the quilts or put much more store by them. There was just too many of them squirreled away in Momma's old trunks or stacked up to the ceiling in closets for a dozen or so to make any difference. And I've never been much for sewing or darning. My hands are just too big and I feel all clumsy and fumble-fingered even if I have to wind a ball of yarn. What I realized sitting on the porch that night listening to Momma and Mr. Van Fleet go on and on was that those quilts would go places I'd never been and see sights I'd never seen, and probably never would. There I was, not able to admit to a soul that a bunch of patchwork quilts made by my grannie and great-aunts and women so long since dead I couldn't recall their names, that a bunch of old quilts had made me but one thing and that was jealous.

Get rid of them all, that's what I wanted to do. Then maybe I'd forget about them and not be made such a fool of. Let them go with Mr. Van Fleet to Delray Beach, Florida, especially if his money is so hot it's burning a hole in his boiler-suit pocket.

"Sell," I suddenly said out loud.

Mr. Van Fleet slapped the arm of his rocker and said, "That's what I've been telling her myself."

Momma just kept on rocking like she hadn't heard a thing.

Mr. Van Fleet finally left when it was good and dark, and we had to loan him a flashlight so's he could see his way to get to his car.

When he was gone, I asked Momma, "You gonna sell him Widow's Mite?"

"I wish I had a nickel for every time you've asked me that. What makes you think I've changed my mind?"

"Because he leaves on Monday," I said. "And this is Saturday."

"That ain't answering my question. What makes you think I have changed my mind?"

She didn't wait for me to say something, because I reckon she knew I didn't have nothing to say. Momma always was the best at calling somebody's bluff. We stood there for awhile in the darkness at the top of the stairs, watching the evening stars come up over Hogback Mountain, not saying a thing.

Finally Momma says Night, Esther, and I say Night, Momma, and that is that.

The next day Moon and his family came for Sunday dinner like they always do. It was Moon and his wife Betty and my two grandbabies, Mandy and Melissa. They had just started school the week before—kindergarten and second grade—and before their Momma and Daddy could even get out of the car they came rushing in with presents they had made for me during craft time. Mandy, the oldest one, brought a turtle she had made out of modeling clay and poked thumbtacks into its back to look like a shell.

"His name is Bill," Mandy said.

"Where should I put him?"

"Up there." She pointed to the shelf on the window above the kitchen sink.

I had to shift pots of African violets and a bunch of old orange juice cans I had wandering jew and coleus rooting in to make room for Bill. I even turned him so he could have a view down towards the valley and the althea hedge.

"Melissa brung something too." Mandy reached for something in Melissa's hand but she jerked away.

"No!"

"Well show it, Melissa."

Melissa lifted those little hands of hers up toward me, and laying there was this funny looking dark, round thing that I thought at first might be a cookie cutter. I picked it up and held it to where the light shone on it. It was a little, hard clay paper weight with Melissa's hand print right in the middle of it. The tips of my fingers would barely fit into the little scoops in the clay her own fingers had made.

I stood there awhile looking at it.

"It doesn't do nothing," Melissa said.

"Yes it does. It sets up here on this window sill next to Bill and looks pretty."

From the kitchen window I could see Moon in the backyard talking to Billy Walkingstick, the old Cherokee who's rented the cabin up above us for as long as I can remember. Moon and Billy had their hands in their back pockets, and every now and then they jabbed at the ground with their shoes. Betty leaned over a bed of petunias and marigolds and pinched off the dead blossoms.

It was times like these I found myself thinking about Cleeve. I should have seen it coming, should have known there was nothing to hold him here. He's not like Moon and Moon's not like Cleeve and I am not the first mother to birth out children who grow up so different you wonder if they can be brothers. Cleeve went and got mixed in with a bad bunch, and one night they went off and beat up an old man. Now Cleeve's down in Raleigh serving out a sentence for assault and battery. I lost something, with Cleeve. And I didn't know how to keep from losing it. It seems like I turned around one day and he was no longer there, like he'd slipped from me, right out of my hands. And right then I felt like I didn't know Cleeve anymore, anymore than I could know that funny looking clay turtle setting in my window sill. But the hurt was still there, I can tell you that.

I kept standing there looking out the kitchen window, leaning up against the cool enamel of the kitchen sink, and for a moment, I forgot where I was.

Then I heard Mandy and Melissa running through the house chasing Momma's six-toed tabby cat and Momma fussing at them. And then Moon and Betty came in the back door loaded down with pound cake and cobbler and okra. This was not time for standing at the sink moping about the way things chose not to turn out.

I gave up my place at the end of the table for Moon like I always did, and Momma sat at the other end. Melissa was still too little to sit in a regular chair, so we put her in the old high chair that her daddy and Cleeve and Mandy had all used. But she was almost too big for it and complained the whole time that it pinched her bottom.

If some stranger had walked in on our Sunday dinner he would have thought we just got through burying somebody. Moon should have felt like the cock o' the walk, what with being the only man there and setting at the head of the table, but I could tell his mind was on losing the sixteen acres and wondering what he could do to add to what he made at International. Betty was her usual quiet self, just chewing her food and looking at whoever happened to say anything.

And me of course. I was thinking about Cleeve, seeing him in some tiny gray room with no window in it.

But Momma was the one I couldn't figure out. What was her cause for setting there like she'd been smote dumb, barely looking at anybody and poking at her food like it might have been last week's oatmeal?

"Momma," I finally said to her when we were by ourselves in the kitchen, "something not suiting you? Why you setting there like death warmed over?"

"I got things on my mind."

"What things?"

"Esther, you act like folks get old and they stop thinking on things. Sometimes I believe I've waited till I got old before I *begun* to do my thinking."

"What's on your mind, Momma?"

"When I finish thinking on it I'll tell you."

And with that she walked back in the dining room carrying a dish of blackberry cobbler and I knew it was no use trying to get it out of her until she was good and ready.

After dinner Moon and Betty took the girls for a walk along the river while Momma and me sat on the front porch in the cane bottom rockers and watched the cars that went down the old highway there in front of the house. Momma was fanning herself with the magazine from the Sunday newspaper, swishing the air around just enough to lift the hair up from the side of her face.

"What you looking at, Momma?" But I knew what she would say, and she did.

"Same thing I look at every time I set on this porch," she said and pointed with the magazine out towards the valley and the mountains. "I reckon I've set here for nearly sixty years. We were setting here that spring evening when the man from Fort Jackson come to tell us about Hollis." My brother Hollis got killed in Korea and the Army sent a man up here to tell us about it. Momma gave the man a piece of pie and a cup of coffee, then went in her bedroom and didn't come out again for two days. About the only time she talks of Hollis is when we set on the porch.

What she said next flummoxed me good.

"I have decided to let Mr. Van Fleet have Widow's Mite."

I stopped rocking.

"I've decided that," she said, like I might not have heard her. She kept looking straight out at the valley and the mountains.

Times like this are strange, I tell you. You expect to leap up and whoop and holler, shouting 'Bout time, 'bout time! But that's never how it turns out with me. I just set there slack jawed and pop-eyed, holding my breath in case it won't last. I could hear my own heart beating, going Widow's Mite, Widow's Mite, Widow's Mite.

I took a few deep breaths and finally said, "What made you change your mind, Momma?"

She kept fanning away. "All of you did," she said. "Moon and the girls, and Cleeve. And you."

"They said something to you?"

"Not a word."

"What you mean they made you change your mind then?"

She finally stopped fanning and looked at me. "You don't learn everything through your ears, Esther. I just set there looking at everybody today, setting where they always do for Sunday dinner. I was missing Cleeve, and thinking about those who've gone. And I decided I was a foolish old woman to try to hold on to one faded old quilt if what money it could bring in could help people setting around the table. Moon's losing land, you've lost Cleeve, why shouldn't I part with Widow's Mite?"

Way out across the highway on the narrow path that runs between the field of corn and an unused pasture, I could see Moon and Betty walking with the two girls. Melissa was up on Moon's shoulders, cupping her hands under his chin like the straps of a helmet. She towered above everybody, even the tassels of the corn, and moved back and forth in a right stately sway. She made me think of a movie I seen once on the television with an elephant carrying an Indian princess who sat in a high-backed golden throne under a canopy of satin and silk the very color of the sunset.

"To be honest, Momma, the money won't matter all that much."

Momma rocked forward fast and brought her heels down on the floor with a clump.

"Just listen to you," she said.

She was right put out with me.

I couldn't sleep that night so I got up and went into the kitchen to make a cup of Sanka and a bread and butter sandwich. Standing at the kitchen window I could see the light on in Billy Walkingstick's cabin and I knew he'd be asleep in his rocking chair with a copy of *National Geographic* spread out over his chest. Billy hardly reads anything else and the ladies in the bookmobile keep him stocked up. It's always struck me as funny to hear an Indian talking about places like Egypt and China and Timbuctoo. But I reckon Billy knows more about strange places in the world than anybody else around. And I know for a fact that he's never been to Delray Beach, Florida, either.

So there I was standing in my and Momma's dark kitchen looking at the light from Billy Walkingstick's cabin and the light from the moon that shone on the backyard and the flower beds and seemed to creep its way up towards me standing at the kitchen window. And up onto the presents from my grandbabies setting there on the window sill.

I picked them both up, in one hand even, they were so small, and brought them up close where I could see them good. They felt cool and I rubbed them against my forehead like folks like to do with a cold drink bottle. They still smelled like children do, sweet and sour at the same time. And they made my heart take a funny leap like I could have knocked down dead anyone who came in and tried to take them away from me.

Momma was right: You do have to get old before you do some thinking about some things.

Momma and I didn't say nothing to each other but we both knew he would show up at his usual time, just after supper but before the sun went down. For a man from Florida he seemed to like to do all his visiting in the dark. But I reckon he needed most of his daytime to look at golf balls and tennis balls and to shop in antique stores.

Something else Momma and I did without saying nothing to each other was dress up. Momma had on her lavender and beige polyester she's worn for the last couple Easters, and Grannie's mourning brooch. I could even see the corner of one of her special Irish linen handkerchiefs sticking out from under her sleeve. I put on my one good summer suit and the beads Mandy and Melissa had given me the Christmas before. It was like we both knew something important was going to happen.

We sat down on the porch to wait, not saying anything about each other's dress-up clothes, not even looking at each other hardly. It kind of made me feel the way you do when you see a man with his zipper down.

About fifteen minutes before sundown we see the lights from the car turn into our driveway, and pick and creep its way up to our house.

"Top of the evening to you." Mr. Van Fleet stood at the bottom of the porch steps, waiting for someone to invite him up. He had on khaki pants and a matching khaki jacket like hunters wear, with big pockets and a belt and little flaps on the shoulders.

If he'd had on one of those funny helmets he would a looked like somebody straight out of Africa.

"Evening," me and Momma said. We went on rocking.

"The last night in the mountains is always a sad time. This time tomorrow I'll be in the panhandle of Florida, sweltering in the heat and fighting off the bugs." He put one foot up on the first step. "You folks are lucky, do you know that?"

"We know that," Momma said.

"And I couldn't go without telling my favorite friends up here good-bye." He moved his foot up to another step. "That, and to come make one more offer to you for Widow's Mite, Molly. I'm even going to up it." And he reached into one of those big pockets in his jacket and brought out a long envelope. "Here's four hundred dollars. In cash—I thought you'd prefer cash. What do you say?"

Momma wasn't looking *at* him, but above him, towards the valley and the river. I was about to say something when she finally said, "I say all right."

Well, Mr. Van Fleet's face cracked into the biggest smile I'd ever seen on anybody and he let out a funny little sound like Hah, and came bounding up the stairs like he was going to grab Momma and the chair she was setting in.

I stood up real fast.

"My momma has given you the wrong impression," I said, putting myself between him and Momma. "We have decided not to sell Widow's Mite. In fact, we have decided not to sell anymore quilts at all."

He craned around me trying to see Momma and saying "Molly, will you—Molly, wha—Molly?"

"You are welcome to come and visit us anytime you're in these parts, but don't be asking for more quilts."

Mr. Van Fleet kept on sputtering away, saying things about having come to a decision, about being reasonable, and such like. And Momma the whole time wasn't saying nothing. Finally I heard her stand up. She put her hand on my shoulder and sort of turned me around. She stood there staring at me in the twilight, her face poked up right next to mine.

"Molly, let's try to keep this between you and me," Mr. Van Fleet said. One thing's for sure, he wasn't too happy by this time. He even tugged at her sleeve a little, like a whiny little boy might do.

But Momma paid him no heed, just kept looking at me until at last she smiled like I hadn't seen her smile in a long time.

Mr. Van Fleet saw it too, and backed down the stairs a little bit. He stopped talking too.

"Mr. Van Fleet," Momma said, drawing herself up, "my daughter is right. I am sorry I misled you. Old women sometimes do foolish things." She set back down in her chair and stared out above his head again. "You drive safely tomorrow. You've got a long trip ahead of you."

He kept going But, but, but, but, sounding like a little motor boat, and flapping his hands around in the air. I felt sorry for him, I did. It seemed like he was more than just a long way from home.

He finally walked on down the stairs and out to his car. He slammed the door so hard it left a little echo in the air. I have to admire him for waiting to get good and angry.

Momma and me went on rocking. The evening star was up in the west, and the katydids were setting up their racket all around us. If Momma'd said anything she'd had to a shouted almost to have herself heard. So she set there not saying a word, because there's times, it seems to me, when it's best to just set. Billy Walkingstick would agree. He hisself says sometimes he sets and thinks, and sometimes he just sets.

And so we just set. A couple of old women looking out at the darkness and listening to the summer sounds, and grateful for a big old house with a good view.

The Changes
Fionna Perkins

In July I was back home. The border of poplars, the locust in Mother's flower garden and the willow in front of the framing for the house we never had money to finish had leafed into shimmering greens. The bluebells were in bloom, and the scarlet and pink and purple petunias spilled over the rock terrace we'd built our first summer in Hillview Acres. Peas and new potatoes the size of marbles were ready to eat. But the cow had been sold, and the electricity was off.

At breakfast my first morning Dad asked if I wanted to pick the raspberries again this year. "Good crop," he said. "Any you sell, the money's yours."

"Sure," I said, beaming, remembering that last summer I made enough for dress goods and new shoes for Mother.

This way I wouldn't have to take another job doing housework to buy clothes for school. Our last had been a real bad winter, worse than the ones before, Dad with no work and Mother seeming off somewhere, and at school in Latin and geometry my brain had stalled. I quit and took a job, but after sweeping and mopping all spring, I wanted to go back and finish high school so I could go on to college.

Dad went out to keep on with the irrigating. As I stood up to clear the table, Mother bounced over and gave me a hug, then held me at arm's length.

"Let me look at you," she said, all smiles and her black eyes sparkling. "I've missed my girl. You've grown, and you're thinner."

"I worked a lot, Mama, about all the time." We sat back down for a visit, and I said, "How's everything?"

"A little better now. Dad has work starting next week at the Olney ranch, and Brodie was hired to clerk at the feed store. First thing he did, he and Nancy ran off and got married, and they're living in town."

"Where's Wallace?"

"Logging on Black Mountain. Juana's with him."

"Heard from Laurel?"

At mention of my sister a shadow clouded Mother's eyes. Laurel, the oldest, had been gone from home a long time and seldom wrote but occasionally sent a box of clothes she was tired of.

For answer Mother opened and closed her clasped hands and said, "Your cat, Feisty, sure missed you."

I was on my way out the next morning with a bucket dangling from my waist and a crate to dump the berries in when I remembered what I'd meant to ask her.

"Where did Hettie Temple go after she was in the hospital?"

"Back to her mother, I guess."

"Hettie's mother died. That's why she came to live with her father and stepmother."

"I don't know, Freda, only that she wasn't to be with Mrs. Temple again ever."

"But isn't Mrs. Temple in the insane asylum at Sweetdale?"

"She was the last I heard," said Mother.

Walking to the berry patch, I thought about Hettie, remembering the other kids at school making fun of her thick woolen socks and long skirts and the twang of her hill speech. If it was like everybody said, that insanity was inherited, Hettie was lucky one way; Mrs. Temple wasn't her real mother.

I didn't like to think of what had happened to Hettie and put my mind on berry picking. Dad had been right. We'd never had a crop like this. Every bush was a mass of white blossoms, green berries, pink berries and ripe berries. It took me two days to pick

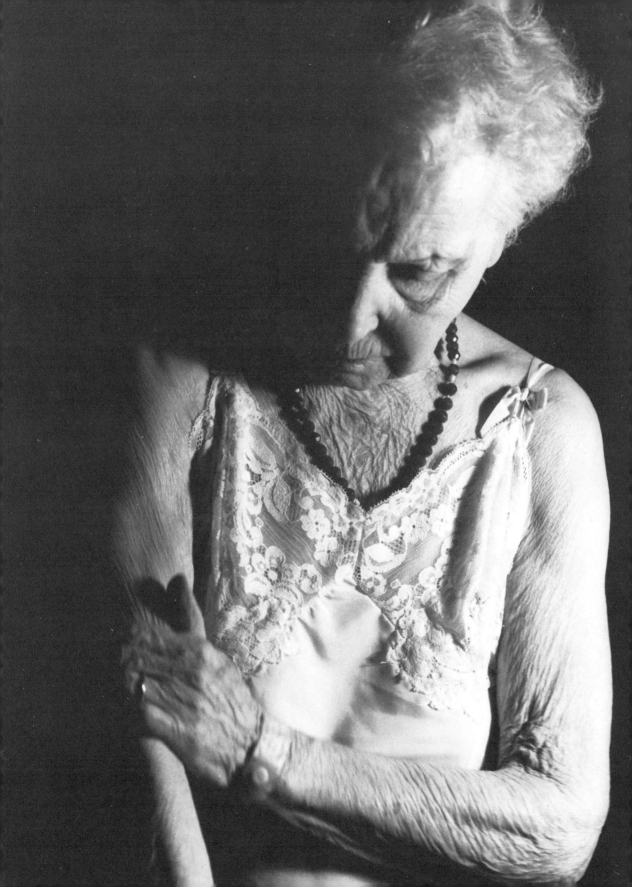

halfway through the patch. By the time I was to the last bush, enough more berries had ripened that I had to start over.

Before I could sell any, I had to pick our share, so every so often I took a filled crate in for Mother to can and make into jam and jelly. Near the end of the week, as I reached the stoop, I heard Dad's voice from inside, loud as though he was angry, saying, "...old enough to be on her own. Face it, Edith. We might have a chance if we sell out and go somewhere else."

I was fifteen. If he was talking about me, that meant back to mopping floors and no school in the fall. It's what we'd done for years, move from place to place, and I didn't think Mother wanted to go back to that. Where we lived was just a shack, but the land was ours, and we had the start of a nice house that was Mother's dream.

Not hearing anything more, I went on in. Dad looked up with a scowl, and Mother seemed pretty upset.

Sunday evening Dad tossed his knapsack into the pickup and drove off for the Olney ranch somewhere to the east about 50 miles. With him gone and the stillness and dusk settling around us, Mother and I, who only talked when we had something to say, didn't speak at all.

She was already at work when I got up in the morning, boiling sheets and washing our clothes by hand. While I picked, she canned. The shack with its one thickness of boards was sweltering. At our evening meal Mother's place was bare of even a glass, and she looked tired and preoccupied.

"Don't you feel good, Mama?"

"I'm fasting."

"Raw eggs and beef scrapings?"

She just smiled. She'd tried that one on me the spring I whooped for weeks. It was from a book we had called *The Ralston Method,* which recommended fasting to rid the body of poisons. I suspected that Mother fasted as much to keep her

Lori Burkhalter, Untitled

weight down as to stay healthy because Dad didn't like her to be fat. Usually she didn't eat for a day or two and drank juice and lots of water.

In the morning she was out irrigating her flowers but again at the wood stove in the afternoon, making jam and ironing our clothes with the heated flatirons she used when we couldn't pay the light bill. Little rivers of sweat ran down her face.

Out in the berry patch I wore a halter and shorts from Laurel's last box of castoffs. If I got too hot, I went to the well back of the shack and filled up on cold water and stood awhile in the shade. But mostly I just picked. Clouds of bees crawled and buzzed around my hands, and I was never stung. I liked bees, and I liked picking; it left my mind free to travel.

While moving from bush to bush, I zoomed off in my head in a movie-star wardrobe, driving my new Cord, which I'd only seen a picture of in a magazine, being a foreign correspondent in China and Paris or autographing the books I intended to write, which everyone wanted to buy.

Then coming back to earth on our two acres in Hillview, I'd take more raspberries to Mother's long workbench. I was used to her being quiet in a warm, comfortable way, humming to herself and smiling when I appeared. This afternoon she didn't smile or look up, and I hadn't heard her sing once since Dad left.

"Sure hot," I grumbled and rubbed sweat off my face. "You drinking juice?"

"No."

"Water?"

Mother shook her head, and I felt a prickle of fear. She'd been a nurse and was hipped on the body's need for water by the quart. In summer around Middleton the only things that didn't burn up and die without being watered were juniper, sagebrush and jackrabbits.

"You'll get sick, Mama."

"It's the way I'm to do it this time."

I went back to the berry patch thinking that she'd never done a fast like this before and that something seemed to be pressing on her mind. A little black ball of worry bounced into my daydreams.

At noontime on Thursday I dangled on the workbench eating a slice of bread and fresh jam and watched Mother living somewhere else. I spoke up so she'd hear me.

"Drinking water now, Mama?"

"I'm to abstain from all food and drink for three weeks." Suddenly she flung her arms wide. "I've had a wondrous vision, Freda."

I looked at her askance; our family was already overrun with visionaries. We imagined Christmases in a house that was only stud walls on a stone basement, trips we never went on and noble deeds of Scottish ancestors centuries dead. Dad envisioned better governments and political systems, and all of us, even Mother, were haunted in the midst of the Depression with a vision of better days.

"What kind of a vision?"

"God is calling his people home."

With a look of rapture Mother pointed to the tapestry sent us after Grandmother died, which hung over the studs on the back wall above her sewing machine.

"The lost tribes of Israel," she said in a hushed voice. "God showed me a vision in the tapestry. I saw all the vanished tribes gathering and moving together. I was among them. We were on our way to the Promised Land. I have to be ready, cleansed and purified."

Was this like the stories I'd read of Joan of Arc's *voices*? As I stared at the shadowed tapestry, the jousting knights began to move, and I quickly shifted my gaze, not wanting to see any of Mother's lost tribes emerging from the gold and black threads on their way to heaven or Palestine. One of us, I thought, better make sense, as Dad was always admonishing.

The next night I watched Mother at her cleansing, and my back hair lifted. She stood in the round tin washtub pouring streams of cold water over her body without a quiver. Her skin just seemed to sop it up. Her wild, fiery eyes burned holes in my head. I stared back, speechless.

A week of her fast was nearly over. By tomorrow evening Dad would be home, and I was sure he'd put a stop to whatever madness had taken Mother.

He brought a piece of beef for Sunday dinner, which Mother roasted. She made a cream sauce for the little potatoes and new peas, a canned milk and vinegar dressing for the leaf lettuce and sponge cake to go under sweetened, crushed raspberries. I set a place for her, and she said grace but didn't eat. Dad told funny stories about the haying crew, and Mother and I laughed. In the afternoon he drove away in the old pickup.

Monday morning I awoke to heat pressing down; we were in for a scorcher. Mother was at the stove fixing poached eggs when I went to the tin basin to wash. At seeing only one plate, I lost my appetite.

"You've got to start eating, Mama," I pleaded.

She turned, not hearing me, and overnight her eyes had paled to a faded brown. She moved as if she had weights on her arms and legs, and her dress fit like a tent.

With an effort Mother straightened. "We have to get the place cleaned up, Freda. The Sunday school is coming for a picnic Friday."

"*Here*?"

"Yes, it's all planned."

"But, Mama, we can't have that whole bunch at a shack like this. Are we supposed to feed them?"

Her face had that unearthly look. "God will provide, Freda. There'll be a great feast and a miracle."

Now, I was scared. This was something more than a fast.

Mother had taught Sunday school at Calvary Baptist in Middleton for years and at Easter made the kids a special breakfast in the church basement, but never were they invited to our place in Hillview. Cummings were too proud for that.

In a loud voice I said, "You've fasted long enough, Mother."

"No, it lasts till Friday."

She had said no water or food for three weeks. Had she been fasting before I noticed? I had counted on Dad to put an end to it, and now he wouldn't be home again for a whole week. She'd start a task and seem to forget what she was doing. At night I couldn't sleep for trying to decide what I should do. The Olneys might have a telephone, but this was Dad's first job since last fall. Wallace, the one I wanted, was as good as lost driving a Cat somewhere in the woods. My brother Brodie, in town, was closest.

At first sight of Mother in the morning I was afraid to leave her for long enough to walk the five miles to Middleton to find Brodie.

"Why don't you stay in bed, Mama?" I urged.

"We've work to do for the picnic."

Her voice had a whistling sound, and her dimples and rounded cheeks had sunk to hollows; her bones stuck out. Her eyes shifted restlessly, bewildered, as if she were searching for something lost.

Picking would give me a chance to think. Three bushes down a row my only thought was that Mother would die before Friday without water. If the picnic was tied in with her fast, and I could stop it, she might start eating. I walked out of the berry patch, over under the willow in front of the stone basement and the unfinished wood framing sticking into the air and out to the road up to the Gerstles. They had the only telephone around, and I didn't care that Dad said a Cumming should never be beholden.

My fingers shook finding Mrs. Baker's number. I was violating another rule, butting into grown-ups' arrangements, but she was the one in charge of the Sunday school.

Her sticky-sweet voice turned sharp when she heard who I was. "Why on earth are you calling me?"

"About the picnic, the picnic at our place Friday. We can't have it."

"Freda Cumming, did your mother tell you to call?"

"Not exactly." I wished I could lie and say a sentence without stuttering. "Mother's not feeling good."

"But this is only Tuesday. I'm sure she'll be all right by Friday."

I pictured Mother as I'd just seen her and screamed at the deaf woman, *"My mother's sick!"*

Mrs. Baker hung up.

Old Mr. and Mrs. Gerstle had been listening, and I explained that Mother had been fasting and with the heat and no food or water, she was in terrible shape. I hoped they would think of a way to help or come home with me and talk to her, but they only asked questions.

Scuffling down past the Cloud place, I clenched my jaws to keep from bawling and thought of Marie Cloud, Mrs. Gerstle's daughter, and the time her baby had convulsions. They had come in the night for Mother to go with Marie to the hosptial. I began praying to God to make Mother's miracle happen early. But no one came all day.

She was swaying on her feet next morning.

"Please eat something, Mama," I begged. "Drink a little water."

"Not till the Father comes," were the only words she spoke.

By her eyes she didn't know me. As her aimless wanderings began, I followed. She dropped to her knees to pray, struggled up and outside, clinging to the chairs, the table, the walls for support, then back inside to flop a few moments on her bed. The old green smock she wore hung on her like an empty sack, and she had no clothes on underneath, which with Mother was unheard of. I was terrified that any minute she would drop dead at my feet. When I moved too near or reached for her, Mother's vacant mad eyes warned me away.

Hot as it was, she was bound to pass out, yet by afternoon was still on her feet, making her way to the well. She lay across the handle, pumping water to pour over herself, and I watched, numb. How could I make her go inside and lie down? I couldn't hit her; she was my mother.

At last Mother fell and lay gasping on the ground. I bent to help her up, but she pushed me away and got to her feet. Staggering back to the well, she drenched herself again and again. The sopping smock clung to her like wrinkled green skin, gaping open where she had torn at it in her agony. Stumbling, falling to her knees and pulling herself up, she reached the skeleton of the home she had dreamed of for so long. With an arm hooked around a two-by-four, she hung there swaying for the Gerstles on the hill and Marie Cloud across the fence to see. Not once had they been outside all afternoon.

Stepping closer, I peered into Mother's eyes. Whatever demon had been driving her had released its hold. Still, even helpless, she couldn't just collapse and let me carry or drag her inside. To see her brought to this and no one caring, I wished us both dead. Trembling, I held out my hand. She clutched it and let me help her across the dirt yard, up the steps and around the cluttered table past the tapestry to her bed. She lay staring at the rafters, taking air in through her mouth. Her stringy wet hair on the pillow looked black again. In moments she was asleep.

By now it was nearly dusk, already night in the shack. I couldn't think what to do next or where to go for help. It was no use praying. How could I believe in a God that had told my mother to kill herself? Striking a match, I lit the coal oil lamp and started a fire to heat water to wash the dishes, then carried the surplus raspberries to the cooler.

Mother was sleeping, and I was still cleaning up when I heard an old rattletrap pull into the yard. In it were Wallace and Juana. How had he known we needed him?

"Where's Ma?" said Wallace.

"In bed. We have to do something or she'll die."

"I got the doc coming."

Before long a new coupe swung into the yard, the doctor's, and he and Wallace talked together in low tones. Juana stood in the shadows against the wall, silent.

I was still scared, but the worst was over. I went outside for air and was startled by the lights of a third car. Inside were two Baptists I saw only on Sunday, the summer preacher and Mrs. Baker. I wanted to tell her she was a day too late.

"How's your mother?" said the preacher.

"Everything's fine now. My brother's here and the doctor. It's been hot, and she wasn't eating much, that's all." To get rid of them quicker, I said, "I'll run see what the doctor says and come tell you."

Wallace had opened the cretonne curtains that hid our beds and moved the lamp to a chair by Mother's. She was awake and talking, and I hoped she wasn't telling them her vision. The doctor stood over her, his face flushed, and he looked angry. I hesitated a moment, then hurried out to persuade the Baptists to leave. Just as I reached their car the door of the shack slammed. It was the doctor.

I ran over to him to ask, "How is she?"

"The woman's crazy!" he shouted, and his voice could be heard around the world. "She belongs in Sweetdale."

"Don't say that. It's not true. She's my mother."

He shrugged and climbed into his coupe and roared off. The dust drifted back over my face and bare arms. I turned from the watching Baptists and looked up at the hogback that rose black in the night straight up behind Hillview like the clenched hand of God, as it had for a thousand years, a million. From inside I heard the sound of boots. Wallace stalked from the shack carrying Mother wrapped in a blanket. She hung over his arms like a bundle of rags.

The windows still showed black outside when voices roused me. I was in an auto court cabin in Middleton and couldn't even remember leaving home. Juana and Wallace sat at a table with Brodie drinking coffee.

"I no sooner hit Middleton than I heard about Ma on the radio," said Wallace. He sounded old and cold and tired. "Out in the yard naked and starving to death. A neighbor'd called the sheriff."

"Dad couldn't figure it," said Brodie. "When I went out to tell him, he said she was all right Sunday."

Wallace snorted. "Well, she wouldn't eat for the doctor, said she'd had a vision, and it was God's will. She didn't weigh, nothin', seventy pounds, if that. If I hadn't got her to the hospital, Ma'd be dead."

Through the thin walls of the cabin from outside came a sound I'd never heard before, my father sobbing as if all his insides were tearing loose. But when Laurel arrived in the afternoon, hair frizzled and teetering on spike heels and giving me a cold stare, he seemed to have recovered.

"Your mother's in the change," he told her. "She hasn't been herself all winter."

"Wallace said the doctor told him she's insane."

"Happens to a lot of women, Laurel. A year or so ago a woman out at Hillview went the same way and had to be committed."

Listening to them, I learned that Mother had been force-fed in the night and had started eating on her own once Dad had visited her in the morning. I wanted to say that Mother hadn't acted crazy till she'd gone I didn't know how long without water, but I was still too numb and scared, and they never paid any attention to me anyway.

More than once I heard Dad say, "She'll never live through it."

With all their talk of death and insanity, I didn't know what to expect by evening when they let me go to the hospital to see her, if she would be in worse shape than yesterday or maybe I'd be seeing her for the last time.

Mother was in bed but sitting forward with her hands clasped around her knees. Her hair had been washed and fell loose in silvery waves over her shoulders. At sight of her whole family trooping in her gaunt face was radiant.

"Why, here's Freda," she said. "How's my girl?"

I searched Mother's eyes. Wherever she'd been, she was back; the madness was gone. I wanted to sink down beside her and put my head on her shoulder. But the Cummings wouldn't let me close, and in a few minutes Laurel edged me out the door.

"You might upset Mother if you stay too long."

Later, when we were all back at the cabin, Laurel talked a mile a minute. "We can't afford anything private. We can't even pay the hospital. What else can we do? She'll need care for a long time."

They were still talking and drinking coffee when I fell asleep with my clothes on. In the morning I asked to visit Mother again.

"Better for her if you don't," said Laurel.

"She coming home soon?"

"Not for awhile."

Juana fixed breakfast, and afterward Wallace and Laurel and Dad left for the hospital. I helped Juana with the dishes and made the beds. Then she put on another pot of coffee and told stories about her Indian grandmother. I watched the expressions change on her beautiful dark face, heard her hiccupy laugh and didn't know a word she was saying. I listened for footsteps and remembered that it was Mother's day of *feast and a miracle*. She was the only miracle I could think of, that she was alive.

In late afternoon just Dad and Laurel came back.

"How's Mama?"

"Better," said Laurel. Neither she nor Dad would look at me.

"When's she coming home?"

My sister glanced at Juana and Dad, then at me, her eyes cold and her face like a piece of blank paper. "Mother's not coming home. She has to be taken care of."

"Where?"

"Now, Freda—" Laurel's voice sharpened—"don't be hysterical. We don't have money for her anywhere else. She's in the change. It's what happens to women then; they go insane. We just did what's best."

"Mama's gone? Where?"

"To Sweetdale."

Turning my back on them, I went over and stood at a window and stared out at the dreary street in the ugly town. Didn't they understand that Mother's vision wasn't real, that it was just something she'd imagined like my trips around the world being rich and famous? I couldn't believe the Cummings had heeded the unfeeling doctor and sent Mother away without even letting me say good-bye. After awhile I sat off by myself pretending to read a magazine and wished I had my cat for company.

A little later Dad said suddenly, "Do you remember Mrs. Temple, Freda?"

Oh, yes, I remembered Mrs. Temple, going berserk and taking after Hettie with a horsewhip, beating her unmercifully from room to room and out into the yard till Hettie to escape ran to the bathroom and swallowed all of a bottle of poison that burned her around the mouth and down her insides.

"Mrs. Temple came to the train to see your mother off."

I supposed that she, like Wallace and the Baptists, had heard about Mother on the radio. "How'd she get out of the nuthouse?" I muttered.

"She's over her change, been home a month. You'd never think to look at her she'd ever been insane."

But what about Hettie, I wondered. Barely saved and left scarred, would she ever find anyone to marry her or even give her a job?

Dad was on his feet, pacing. "What say we pack up and get on out home?"

Laurel and Juana were coming with us to stay the night. My brother still wasn't back. I'd heard Laurel tell Juana he was the one who signed the papers to send Mother to Sweetdale.

Wallace was probably somewhere getting drunk.

Lori Burkhalter, "Sammy Was a Good Man"

For My Mother

Michele Wolf

I sharpen more and more to your
Likeness every year, your mirror
In height, autonomous
Flying cloud of hair,
In torso, curve of the leg,
In high-arched, prim, meticulous
Feet. I watch my aging face,
In a speeding time lapse,
Become yours. Notice the eyes,
Their heavy inherited sadness,
The inertia that sags the cheeks,
The sense of limits that sets
The grooves along the mouth.
Grip my hand.
Let me show you the way
To revolt against what
We are born to,
To bash through the walls,
To burn a warning torch
In the darkness,
To leave home.

Therese Becker, Red Man Chewing Tobacco

A Place for Mother

Joanne Seltzer

PRELIMINARY ADVICE

Remember how you once went shopping
for the right nursery school
and when the teacher asked you
if your child was toilet trained
you lied and said she was.

Use the same strategy
in shopping for a nursing home.

Later—when you are told
of Mother's incontinence—
you will clench your fist and shout:
"What have you done to my mother?"

MORE ADVICE

Have a daughter-to-mother talk.
Ask her what she wants.
If she doesn't know
ask her if she's happy.
She will either say
she doesn't know
or she will be silent.
Tell her how much you love her.
Promise you won't forsake her.

A CHECKLIST

Place One has an eight-year waiting list.
Place Two has a nursing home odor.
Place Three is in a bad neighborhood.
Place Four is in another city.
Place Five won't take medicaid.
Place Six takes only terminal cases.
Place Seven doesn't offer therapy.
Place Eight puts three in a room.
Place Nine requires a hike to the dining room.
Place Ten demands Mother's money up front.
Place Eleven decides Mother won't fit in.

THE SEARCH

Though Mother says
she won't fit in anywhere
you keep on looking.

You learn about levels of care,
levels of caring.

The Jewish Home offers
a night in the Rabbi's room
when the Rabbi isn't there

to newly matched couples
who hanker after
geriatric sex.

A SUDDEN ILLNESS

When Mother is discharged
from the hospital
you accompany her down
on the same elevator
with a young couple
bringing Baby home.

They call to mind
the Holy Family
until you realize
that every family is holy.

You feel holier-than-thou.

CONFUSION

While you ponder your choices
Mother continues to slip.

She thinks she will go to jail
for being a dope addict.

She thinks there's a conspiracy
against the family.

She worries about the poison
in the drinking water.

Though people call her *lady*
she isn't sure if she's a woman
or a man.

PLATITUDES

Mother is with God.
Mother is at rest.
Mother is with Dad.

Mother was ready to go.
Mother has paid her dues.
Mother is still with us.

Mother loved life.
Mother lived a full life.

Time heals all wounds.
You will mourn Mother
the rest of your life.

THE ORPHAN

There's no umbrella now
to separate you
from eternity.

Meanwhile an army
marches behind you
in the rain.

Your friends are dead
or dying.

You're a survivor
with all the loneliness
of survivorship.

LIFE MUST GO ON

Your hair has turned white.
Your skin is parchment.
You have a bulldog's jowls.

You ask yourself
what Mother's face is doing
in the mirror.

She sticks out her tongue.

You wonder where the years went
and with horror
realize you forgot to flush
the toilet.

IN CONCLUSION

Not wanting to be a burden
on your children
you sign yourself into
a nursing home.

You become active
in every group
and serve on every committee.

You are voted
resident-of-the-month,
a role model.

Mother would be proud of you.

Birthday Portrait in Muted Tones

Dori Appel

In this expanse of pale couches
and bone-colored carpet
the artifacts refuse to age. After
years of sun and heat, they still seem
like new arrivals popped from
cardboard cartons yesterday. The light
shining through the wide windows
makes me giddy. I want to press
bowls and baskets down harder
on their tables, pound chairs
into the rug, give things weight.
My brother sits in what was
once my father's place. His hair
is gray like mine. Here
where we were never children
we rekindle old resentments over
the three-tiered cake. We are
the bad fairies at this celebration,
avenging slights. Our mother,
if she notices, gives no sign.
She smiles as we push our presents
towards her, picks intently
at the wrappings with slow-motion
hands. Reaching from my nearer seat
to help, I see how white her hair is,
bent over the stiff, bright bows.

Old Woman
Billie Lou Cantwell

A time was
when I smiled sweetly
and coddled old women,
listened to their tales
of how it was
when times were
really bad.

Lately, I don't much
like old women
and try to ignore their
clutching tongues.
The times they rub today
chafe my own
recollections
of not so long ago.

A Woman at Forty

Enid Shomer

A woman at forty
stands long at her mirror
as though it were a pool
which could smooth
the distortions of her face.

On the street she walks
as if each step led her
to an altar, and any corner
might straighten out
her life.

She cultivates flowers,
drapes everything with polished chintz.
Among friends she speaks little
but her hands, moving from hair
to lips to lap

tell the same story
as the bit actress
who inadvertently points to herself
as she declaims the entrance
of the queen.

At night she listens for a knock
on the door, though everyone
she knows is asleep.
Through her window stars
which once granted wishes

are burning as they retreat.

New Directions

Susan A. Katz

Outside there is a thin
wind flirting with the trees
it has teased the curtains
into dancing; I keep time
in my head.

Memorizing the seasons, I touch
things as if my fingers
will learn them
again; weary of explanations,
at mid-life I am more comfortable
with the truth.

Outside, the mountain ash hangs
heavy with orange berries,
like overripe breasts they weight
the branches down; I feel
the tug, my flesh molding
itself to gravity; closer now
to the soil than ever
to the sky.

Lori Burkhalter, New Leaf

Late Autumn Woods

Rina Ferrarelli

The press of green over
and the ritual of leaves

the wood has settled
into its prime dimensions
the lines etched in the light
pouring in from all sides.

Forts and nests abandoned,
the trash exposed.

Walking through
I can now see where the main path ends
and the others
branching off like veins on a leaf.

The palm of a hand
with a well-marked lifeline.
A wood thinned of possibilities.

Yet the sky, bluest in the north
and visible only in snatches before,
has opened up all around me,
as if a fog had lifted at last,
a heavy curtain.

Athlete Growing Old

Grace Butcher

The caution is creeping in:
the step is hesitant
    from years of pain;
a soft grunt bends the body over,
    and straightens it.
The skin loosens; everything moves
    nearer the ground.

To overcome the softening,
    the yearning towards warmth,
she exercises,
    makes her muscles hard,
    runs in the snow,
    asks herself when she is afraid,
"What would you do now if
    you were *not* afraid?"

She listens for the answer
    and tries to be
    like that person who speaks,
who lives just outside
    all her boundaries
    and constantly calls her
    to come over, come over.

Body
Lillian Morrison

I have lived with it for years,
this big cat, developed an
affection for it. Though it is
aging now, I cannot abandon it
nor do I want to. I would love
to throw it about in play but
must be careful. It cannot summon that agile grace of old. Yet
it's really pleasant to be with,
familiar, faithful, complaining
a little, continually going about
its business, loving to lie down.

I Know the Mirrors

Janice Townley Moore

I know the mirrors
that are friends,
the ones in semi-darkness that hide
the hard crease of jowl,
or the ones with the correct distance
to fade the barbed wire fence
above the lips. But skin breaks
like dry river beds.
Rooms must become darker,
distance greater.
I grope for a solution,
knowing that no woman
ever looked better with a beard.

Investment of Worth

Terri L. Jewell

You value the earthen vase—
       each crack applauded
       for authenticity,
  a slave's Freedom Quilt—
       hand-pulled stitchery
       a rare tale relinquished,
Victorian silver hair pins
       with filigreed flowers
       delicate as unconscious.
A collector of ancients
       quite proud of your tastes
       but scornful of
              curled brown leaves
              slight gray webs
              parched desert soil
       of a woman
       turned and tuned to her ripening,
              whose life is dear
              as a signed first edition,
              whose death as costly
              as a polished oak bed.

Michelle Noullet, Arriving in Odessa, Texas

Gracefully Afraid

Mary Anne Ashley

I have a friend who never does anything right. I don't mean morally. Socially. What I mean is, she won't be respectful when it could benefit her; she won't flirt; she won't color her hair; she won't lose any weight; she won't dress herself up; she won't wear makeup; she just won't try to get along. She wears the worst damned looking shoes you ever saw.

They're comfortable, she says.

Well, so what, is what I say. Who wants to be around anyone who wears shoes like that? No man wants to walk down the street with a woman who is fifty-two years old, whose hair is turning grey, who is twenty pounds overweight, whose idea of dressing up is a pink sweatshirt, and who wears shoes that look like that.

I personally know of a court case she lost because she refused to call the judge, Sir, or Your Honor, during the *entire* proceeding. I was furious. I could have killed her. I went to a lot of trouble during that case. I drove her to the lawyer's office several times. I listened while she ranted and raved about justice and injustice and the class system. I sat with her through the whole mess. And she blew it. On purpose. I know that's why he decided against her. All that work. All that time. All that energy down the drain. She owed it to her lawyer, she owed it to me, and she certainly owed it to herself to sit up there and act right. She wasn't rude, don't get me wrong. She answered all the questions with a complete and intelligent response, but that's not what we're talking about. I tried to call him Sir and Your Honor a couple of times, she says. I couldn't get it out of my mouth, and that's the truth. Huh! The truth. It still burns me up to think about it. It's not as though she stood there and made a heroic political or social

Therese Becker, Two Grandmas

statement or anything like that.

If she made even the slightest effort with her looks she would be damned attractive. She is now. Almost. In a certain way. But she won't try. And she says that she will never again pay to have her hair cut. That she will never again sit still while someone cuts her hair. So she wears it in a long lank down her back or folded up on her head with two giant bobby pins holding it down. It looks like a big cow plop with straw sticking out.

Don't laugh at my hairdo, she says. I don't like that. Well, I'm not laughing on purpose, just to hurt your feelings, I say. You'd laugh too if you ever looked at it from the back. I don't mean to hurt your feelings but if something is funny, it's funny.

Okay, she says, but I never laugh at your hair.

Well, of course she doesn't. Every hair of mine is in place. I don't set one foot out the door if my hair doesn't look just right. If your hair looks lousy, you look lousy all over. If you look lousy, you feel lousy. The first thing I do after my morning shower is to apply my makeup. Before I do my hair, I apply my makeup.

It's a work of art, she says.

I'll show you how to do it, I tell her. I've told her that a thousand times over the years. Never mind, she says, that's okay. During the time I've known her she must have spent a thousand dollars on nice cosmetics, but she just takes them home and puts them in a drawer. What a waste. She doesn't do that anymore. Thank God. I hate to see that kind of waste.

I love your sense of ritual and discipline, she tells me. It's true. I understand things like that. I wouldn't say that I'm rigid but I do things in a certain way and I benefit from that. You see the results of my work. She works, but you can't see the results. She isn't lazy. Far from it. It's just that she doesn't have a tight routine about anything, and so she does a little of this and a little of that. But nothing shows. No one room in her house is clean on the same day as any other. She is *not* dirty. No way. I couldn't be friends with someone who was dirty or lazy. But her place is always cluttered. Messy. I admit there is a certain charm to it. It gives the impression that she's hard at work on some emotional or intellectual task. Sometimes there is mystery and excitement around her place. I sit on her couch while she's in another room and feel as though she's going to haul out a canvas she's painted in secret. Or she's going to walk in carrying a manuscript she'll slam down on the table. Some literary masterpiece she's written while I wasn't looking. That's one of the things about her I like: she gives the impression that she's somewhere in the wings, doing great, creative work. Or that she's behind the scenes developing a new school of philosophical thought. Of course, that's not the reality. The reality is that she's in her advancing middle age, with no good job, no steady job, with an almost-college degree which is worse than no degree at all because she has no money to go back to school. And besides, by the time she gets back to school, if she ever does, they'll have changed all the requirements so that she'll have to start all over again, and all her past work will have been for nothing. The reality is that she's headed for complete disaster. (She doesn't even own an iron. She says she did something with it, but can't remember what!) Sometimes she can't pay the rent; sometimes she can't feed her animals; and sometimes she doesn't have one thin dime in her pocket. I worry about her a lot. But it's her own damned fault.

Don't worry about me, she says, it's not helpful.

I can't help worrying about you.

Then it's your problem, not mine.

Well, that's gratitude for you. Thanks a lot, I tell her. Don't call me up the next time you need money for dog food, and don't turn to me when you need a ride job-hunting. Just don't call on me.

Okay, I won't, she says.

Don't, I say.

Now that that's settled, she says, let's talk about something else. Let's talk about you for a change. I know what. Let's go for a drive to Bodega Bay. I'll pay for the gas.

We'll charge it on her gas card, she means. Through the worst of times, she's held onto that. She was homeless once. Literally. Out in the streets, but she had that card. It's my ticket to ride, she says.

We love to go for drives. We see the same sorts of things. Along the Russian River, out to Jenner or up the coast to Fort Ross, or up the Napa Valley. When she had some money, we drove to Vacaville for dinner at the Nut Tree once a week. When we could stand the traffic, we drove to Berkeley to the Claremont Hotel, or to Normans to eat giant artichokes and walnut pie.

She was a sharp dresser. I felt good walking up the street with her. Not now. She is not one of those women who can throw on rags and look like a million. But one thing that makes me feel good about myself is that, embarrassed or not, I am the kind of person who does not abandon another person because of what she wears or doesn't wear. It's uphill work a lot of the time. Sometimes though, it's fun when we go someplace nice and I'm dressed up and she's not. It's bold and defiant. I feel like people envy my courage and loyalty. Other times, it's not fun at all. It's downright humiliating. I feel she's asking too much of our long friendship. More and more I feel that way.

We're getting older and we should try our best. But she says, No, I did that for forty years. That's half my life. She said that right after she had a dream that she was going to live to be eighty-one. We tell one another our dreams. We like our dreams. We feel friendly toward them, even when they are a little frightening. It's a bond between us. We're both relaxed about what our unconscious minds might cough up during the night. After she told me that dream, she said, Now, that's it. The next forty years are mine. I said, Good for you! I had no idea she was talking about not wearing skirts anymore, about letting herself go.

She used to have a beautiful body. Now it's hidden under those twenty extra pounds. Mine is out there, highly visible. You've got a great body, she says. Well, I ought to, I reply.

I work darned hard to keep it that way. I work out in the gym every day. There's not an ounce of fat on me. I run every day. When she runs, she wets her pants. That's not her fault. I know that. She's had kidney infections since she was young. But she could do yoga. But she won't. She even likes yoga. She used to do it with her daughter-in-law. It's getting down on the floor and being out of this world that she says she doesn't like. So, she's flabby and I'm not. I'm fifty-one years old and still look great. Like it or not, we get more high marks when we look good in bathing suits.

We both read the same books, and I understand feminist principles. But what is, is. We have to get along in the here and now. This is a man's world and until that changes, we have to do certain things. We have to say certain things; we have to look a certain way. Like it or not. When she kicks up a fuss, I tell her she's just kicking the slats of her cradle.

You know, it's funny. When we first met eighteen years ago, she didn't know beans about being angry or getting revenge or having a good toe-to-toe fight. That's one of the things she liked about me. You don't pretend to any of the virtues, she said. You get even when someone does you dirt, and you don't have fits of remorse about it. I like that about you. You know that anger doesn't kill. I know it too, but I still don't know how to use it. You said *that* to *them*? she'd ask, her eyes popping.

Sure I did, I'd say. So what?

I love the way you say, So What.

When we first met, she'd never given anyone the finger. Hardly swore at all. She couldn't get mad without saying, I'm sorry.

Once, when she was sick, I gave her my favorite book on anger, how to express it. She read it, and came off the couch like she was shot from guns. She loved it. She loved it that I gave that book to her. You could say I had a big hand in the kind of person she is today. She's a great one to have in your corner when there's a fight.

But as we get older, I get nervous about what she'll do next. I say, Please don't make a fuss. She says, Don't call sticking up for ourselves making a fuss. Besides, even if we make a fuss, what can they do to us? They've done just about all they can do. I'll never be a history professor and you'll never be a Hollywood screen writer. We're just pokey people now, getting old, in our pokey places. For God's sake, let's not go to our graves without at least shooting our mouths off, she shouts.

And let's not go to our graves, I shout back, without you looking pretty for at least one day. I can hardly bear to look at you anymore.

She hung up. Who can blame her? I shouldn't have said that. It was mean. If I feel that way about her I shouldn't pal around with her any longer. It's not fair. It's not just a whim, the way she is. Not some stage she's going through. She's not going to change back. I see that. I'd drop her tomorrow. I think about it all the time. But she's fun to be with, like something funny or special or exciting is about to happen. Sometimes people envy me because she is my friend and not theirs. She's attractive in some elusive way. But it makes me furious.

We didn't talk for over three months after she hung up on me. I missed her. But it was a relief not to see her. Not to deal with her anger and insights. Just do my daily routine: relax, read novels, drift, and windowshop. Sightsee and be seen. Pick the daisies and smell the roses, as the old saying goes. But then I thought, Dammit, I want to see her, want to talk to her because there's something I have to say. So, I called her. We got together, had a good time. But things were never going to be the same. We discovered that we could be content not seeing each other for long periods. What a relief.

What we differ about most is what is most important: our dignity. The important thing is respect. How do you get respect when you have that gut hanging down over your belt, and you wear those damned lace-up shoes? Your hair's a mess, and you obviously don't respect yourself. So, how do you expect anyone to respect you? I ask her.

And how can you consider yourself dignified with cleavage like that? she says. How can you respect yourself when you dose your head with dangerous chemicals every six weeks. You're over fifty-years-old, for God's sake, and you bat your eyes like some silly fifteen year old. You spend half your life in front of the mirror. That's not my idea of dignity.

Maybe I do, I say, but I get the good jobs, don't I? I'm not the one who can't pay the rent. I'm not the one who's sick with money worries half her life. The *last* half of her life. Let's be clear about that. You don't even smile at anyone anymore. You still have to live in this world, you know. So what kind of respect are you getting for your trouble? Maybe every two years someone writes from Florida or Washington or God knows where and says he or she likes the story you wrote, but that's only one story. The only story you ever published, and I hate to throw that up to you because I think you're a wonderful writer. You know I do. But you aren't going to get published anymore. You haven't published a story in five years. And you are never going to get your degree, and we both know that because you have a crummy attitude. So, where is all this respect that you work so hard to get? Go on, show me. Correct me if I'm wrong, but I don't see any of it lying around here. There isn't any manifested in your refrigerator. You don't even have margarine, for crying out loud. Sometimes you just have to kiss ass, for God's sake. You know that. Tap into reality for just ten lousy seconds!

I don't mean that. We end up yelling. It bothers me. She's very political, very realistic. I say it because I'm mad at her, and I worry about her. It's like having a friend who has a disease that is helped with medication, and then the friend won't take the medication, and you get mad. It's like that. The disease we both have is being born women into a man's world. It's not a nice disease, and it's a progressive disease, but you don't have to die from it. It doesn't have to be fatal. It's like she's turning a disease that's only chronic into a disease that's fatal. And that's scary.

Well, I've just about had it. I love her, and I know she loves me. I love all the fun we've had over the years, and I love the times we've helped each other out of jams and through bad times. But I *don't* want to write protest letters to wardens of women's prisons. I want to write shopping lists. Expensive shopping lists. I want a nice house and pool to sit by, reading or daydreaming, maybe in St. Helena. I've wanted that for all the years I can remember. I want a husband who is financially secure and generous, who is affectionate. One who won't invade my space. In return for what he gives, I'll give him good meals, good sex, and clean, pressed clothes. That's not such a terrible contract, is it? It would be comfortable and peaceful. But I could never trust her in that kind of environment. Not that she'd be rude. But she couldn't be trusted. Something bad would happen.

It shames her and makes her mad, she says, the way I hang around the golf course, the tennis courts. But I play golf, dammit, and I play tennis, and that's where I'm going to find a St. Helena man. Just because I haven't found one during the past twenty years proves nothing, no matter what she says. It only proves that I haven't found him yet; not that I won't. And when I do find him, she won't be an asset. I take that back. Men like her. She makes them laugh so she'll seem an asset until they get to know her. After that, they'll think she's a Communist. And I'll be tarred with the same brush, and I'll kiss that house and pool goodbye. Please don't recoil as though I'm some kind of monster, because I'm not. I'm a woman who will be in her sixties in just ten short years. A woman with practically no value anywhere in this world, so I don't intend to be in this world. I intend to be in the small world of the Napa Valley. I intend to grow old gracefully, and you can't grow old gracefully if you've spent the last half of your life swimming against the current the way she has. I want to grow old surrounded by pretty things. And I can't do that if I'm worn out with worry because I have a friend who lands in fleabag flophouses, who lives in poverty, who might get hauled off to prison for associating with terrorists, who could die in a ditch because she has no home. I can't look forward to that. I won't. Sometimes now, when she's talking, my attention fades, and I look at her and think, you're going to blow my old age, you old bat. And I hate that.

Last week we went to a powwow at the American Indian University near Davis. I feel lucky to have a friend who was invited to a powwow. I'm glad I went with her. Not that I had a good time. I didn't, but it was an experience that goes into my brain bank. And that enriches me. Next week, I'm taking her to Sebastopol to interview an old woman who was the first female member of the ILWU in Petaluma. That will be interesting. I'm looking forward to it. But it's scary too because I think this old woman's a Communist. Don't worry about it, she says, everyone was a Communist in those days. But I do. What if it came out ten years from now that I spent the afternoon at the home of a Communist? What then? That would put me into the worst kind of light when I could least afford it. I don't intend to grow old with that kind of fear.

I don't intend growing old, living on the brink of disaster, frantic and anxious, the way she is most of the time. Don't kid yourself.

I'm a thin-ice skater, she laughs.

It's not funny, I say. That's not something to be proud of.

I don't want to be called from poolside one nice day to bail her out of some two-bit Central Valley jail. I don't want to explain to my future husband that he has to attend the Beaulieu Vineyard Concert-Under-The-Stars alone because I have to drive down to Oakland to attend to a batty old woman who was found raped and beaten in a downtown alley, and who managed to whisper my name and phone number before lapsing into a life-threatening coma. I just won't do it.

So, I've made up my mind. After our get-together next week, I'm going to slip over to her place early in the morning. Before dawn. Leave all of her books I've borrowed on the front porch.

I don't want to do it that way. But I have to. She'll know what it means. I'm going to miss her like crazy. She'll miss me, too. But that's too bad — too bad to end it like that.

But my mind's made up. It comes under the heading: Old Age Security.

words never spoken

Doris Vanderlipp Manley

walking through the city I saw the young girls
with bodies all silk from underthings to eyebrows
legs shaven
heels pumiced
nails glossed
hair lacquered
thighs taut
eyes clear
gladbreasted tittering girls

and I wondered how even for an hour
you could love a woman who has no silk
no silk
only burlap
and that
well worn
tattered
and frayed
with the effort of making a soul

Clearing the Path
Elisavietta Ritchie

My husband gave up shovelling snow
at forty-five because, he claimed,
that's when heart attacks begin.

Since it snowed regardless, I,
mere forty, took the shovel, dug.
Now fifty, still it falls on me

to clean the walk. He's gone on
to warmer climes and younger loves
who will, I guess, keep shovelling for him.

In other seasons here, I sweep
plum petals or magnolia cones
to clear the way for heartier loves.

Dear Paul Newman

Marie Kennedy Robins

After all these years
it's over between you and me.
There's a younger man.
I get to see him five times a week
and he tries to bring me the world.
I worried a lot about your racing
in them fast cars, your beer drinking,
the fact that the color of your eyes
is fading a little with age.
Them eyes always reminded me of Ed Kozelka
who sat next to me in American History.
When you and Ed turned them blues on me,
it sure made my pilot light blaze up.
When reporters asked why you was
faithful to Joanne, you once said,
"Why should I go out for hamburger
when I can have steak at home?"
Now that Joanne is looking so plain,
I wonder if you are going to Wendy's.
Paul baby, it was fun, and
I'll never forget your spaghetti sauce.
I gotta move on.
I'm the same age as you, but in the dark
Peter Jennings will never notice.

Reaching toward Beauty

Hyacinthe Hill

Your love declines. You, thinking little lines
around my eyes are fallen lashes, try
to brush them off. I do exfoliate.
In this autumn of my being, parts of me
fly, like tossed and wintry-blasted leaves.
I don't regret their passing. I must work
to make a clean and crystal-perfect form.
I, alchemist, and I, philosopher's stone,
have sacrificed the fat, and froth, and fur
of youth, to walk through fire, leap in the dark,
swim inward rivers, pray at a wailing wall.
The wrinkles, sags, the graying hair are earned.
You mourn like a child over a broken doll.
Only the core of this crone was ever real.

Love at Fifty

Marcia Woodruff

We come together shy as virgins
with neither beauty nor innocence
to cover our nakedness, only
these bodies which have served us well
to offer each other.

At twenty we would have dressed each other
in fantasy, draping over the damp flesh,
or turned one another into mirrors
so we could make love to ourselves.

But there is no mistaking us now.
Our eyes are sadder and wiser
as I finger the scar on your shoulder
where the pin went in,
and you touch the silver marks on my belly,
loose from childbearing.

"We are real," you say, and so we are,
standing here in our simple flesh
whereon our complicated histories are written,
our bodies turning into gifts
at the touch of our hands.

A Letter from Elvira

Bettie Sellers

I saw your picture in the local news;
since you look like a nice lady,
I am writing you to find me

a princely widower, one who will appreciate
my three-college mind, the delicate lace
of my crochet, the gourmet taste of my cuisine.

He would need a house,
French Provincial would be nice,
grey or maybe a forest green.

And a dog too, but not a boxer —
I don't like the way they look at me,
like these Methodists here in Baysville.

The preacher said I was reaching too high
and who would marry me anyhow. Some of them
are in drugs, the Mafia, you know,

and most of the Baptists are perverts.
The Board of Education is worse; they say
I'm too old to be teaching their children.

I enclose my picture, and my telephone number.
Have him call anytime; I'll be here.
I remain, yours very sincerely, Elvira Wade.

Tin of Tube Rose

Sandra Redding

I remember Mama sitting with that can of snuff clutched in her hand, just dipping and rocking, not a care in the world. Mosquitoes and flies would buzz right up in her face but, as long as she had a pinch of snuff in her mouth, she wouldn't even give them a swat. She'd just sit there, that glazed look in her eyes. Once, I asked, "Mama, what in tarnation goes on in your mind when you're dipping?"

After spitting in that Kentucky Fried Chicken bucket she always kept close by, she answered. "Can't explain it, Lizzie. Maybe you ought to try it and find out for yourself."

Now I wasn't uppity but I had no intention of trying snuff, but all that was before Ed died. A death can change a body's mind about a lot of things.

Ed was my husband. We'd been married going on forty years. The night he died, we were sitting in front of the TV arguing about those girls on "Charlie's Angels." Ed said, "That blond's a real charmer, ain't she Lizzie?"

Well, I didn't agree with him, so I told him what I thought. Before you could say *peaturkey,* an empty can of Budweiser came rolling right over to my foot. At first, I thought Ed had thrown the fool thing at me for saying the blond he liked was skinny and conceited but when I looked over at the recliner, he was slumped down just like all the air had been let out.

Doc Hollins said it was Ed's heart. "He couldn't have picked an easier way to go," Doc told me. Ed didn't feel much pain and it was over real quick.

That night, I got in touch with the children, all eight of them scattered over six states. "A family's no count," Ed used to say, "unless they stick together when the going gets rough." Well, I reckon we showed our worth cause every last one of them kids—even Eva Jane who lives way out in Oregon—managed to get there to see their daddy be put away.

The viewing was two days later at Thompson's Mortuary. By the time we got there, the place was already full of folks. Many of them I'd never seen before. Vergil Peters—he runs the flower shop down at the end of Main Street—must have had a special going on pink carnations cause they were stuck in every sort of wreath and basket. Why they smelled so sickly sweet they could have suffocated King Kong. It's always seemed to me that death deserved a healthier smell than them hothouse flowers, but Ed was dead and people had shown their respect by sending pink carnations and there wasn't one earthly thing I could do about it.

If the flowers weren't bad enough, people were staring at me. Now I'm not used to being stared at. I knew they were waiting to see me cry, but I'm not much of a crier. Fact is, the only time I ever shed more than a tear or two was when Rhett Butler told Scarlett O'Hara, "Frankly, my dear, I don't give a damn" in *Gone With the Wind*, which I managed to see all six times they showed it at the Rand Theater. Still, everybody expected it so to oblige them, I touched a Kleenex to my eyes, pretending. Then I bent over the casket and took one last look at Ed.

They'd put paint on his face. I could tell. And they'd dressed him in a dark blue suit that wasn't at all becoming. Why I couldn't even remember the last time I'd seen Ed Chalmers in a suit. Oh, he had a plaid sports coat that he'd wear to Moose Lodge dances, but he'd have never worn anything as drab as that outfit they were putting him away in. I pinched one of the carnations from a wreath that had a plastic telephone fastened to it, the purple banner across the front proclaiming, "Hello, Jesus." Though I tucked the flower in Ed's buttonhole, it still didn't do much to brighten him up. I wanted the Ed I remembered, the Ed I'd bedded down with for most of my life. "Ed," I whispered so nobody else would hear, "why'd you up and die? I was just hitting my prime."

Now some folks might argue that fifty-eight is past prime for a woman, but I was forty-four before I had my last baby. To tell the truth, I was beginning to suspect there wasn't anything more to life than a dirty diaper. When most women I knew were going out to get jobs at the K-Mart and Winn-Dixie, I still had runny-nosed younguns pulling at my skirt tail. But don't think that ever stopped Ed Chalmers. He married me with one thing on his mind and for all I know, he died thinking about it as well.

Right after the fifth one was born, I had a serious talk with Doc Hollins. "Doc," I said, "how about writing me a prescription for saltpeter so I can put some in Ed's coffee?"

Doc almost laughed his grey mustache off. "That's a good one," he said.

"What do you mean, that's a good one?"

For just a second, he looked puzzled. "You do know, Lizzie," he finally said to me, "that there's no such thing as saltpeter."

Well, I didn't know. I'd heard about it all my life and I couldn't figure out why folks would talk so much about something that didn't exist. I wanted to ask Doc Hollins about something to prevent babies but I didn't. I was afraid he would start laughing again.

After the sixth baby, Mama started complaining. "Lordy, Lizzie," she said, trying to talk around the snuff in her mouth, "looks like you could keep your legs together."

I tried but Ed pried them apart before that youngun was six weeks old. "Ain't no use yelling," he told me. "The sheriff won't arrest a man for raping his own wife."

Now I don't want you to think I had anything against sex. Fact is, I probably liked it just as much as that blond on

"Charlie's Angels," but I was tired—tired of having babies, tired of eating pinto beans.

I've heard it said that every dog has its day and I reckon that's true. Mine came after I went through *the change*. That unopened box of Kotex sitting on the bathroom shelf became my flag of freedom. Some women complain that a hot flash is embarrassing but, far as I'm concerned, it's not half as embarrassing as walking around all your life with a belly full of baby.

After *the change*, the children started growing up, one by one, and fending for themselves. For the first time in years, I had money for lipstick and dangling earrings. Why, I even bought myself a pair of fake eyelashes. Ed liked it. He liked it just fine. We joined the Moose Lodge and started going to dances on Friday nights. Saturday nights were extra special. While I bathed, Ed would look at pictures in his *Penthouse* magazine. Then we'd light the red heart-shaped candle that Sybil Ann, our eldest, gave us for Christmas.

Those were good years and there could have been more of them if Ed hadn't up and died. Being a widow ain't easy, I'll tell you that. I missed Ed. I missed him terrible. Much as I'd criticized him, calling him a sex pervert back when he kept getting me pregnant, there was nothing that I wouldn't have done to have him back in that oak bed with me. Oh, I smiled and acted respectable in public but inside, I just churned for a man.

For a while, I didn't think about other men—only Ed. I remembered how he'd smelled of Aqua Velva and how black hairs, as well as a few grey ones, sprouted curly over his chest. But before long, I started noticing other men. Young men. Old men. It didn't matter none. I'm ashamed to admit it, but I lusted after all of them. Once I bought six rolls of paper towels just because they were wrapped up in the picture of a handsome mustached fellow. By then, I knew things had gone too far. "Lizzie, old girl," I told myself, "you better do something before you make a fool of yourself."

Before I'd even had a chance to figure out what I ought to do, I got a telephone call from Flora Mae Simmons. "You better get yourself to the revival meeting going on down at Shiloh Baptist Church." That's what Flora Mae said. I'll tell you, it gave me a real spooky feeling getting that call. It was just as if she knew all those wild thoughts were flying through my head. Now, I'm a believer. Always have been. But with all them kids to tend to, I'd gotten out of the church-going habit. After Flora Mae's call, I decided it was high time I got started back.

That night in the dimly lit church, I did my best to concentrate on what the preacher was saying as he stood there proclaiming the word of God with flashing white teeth, his voice all full of passion. When he shouted about sin and damnation, his pink, wet tongue flicked in and out of his mouth. I started wondering what he'd look like with his clothes off. I couldn't help myself. Wicked thoughts just flooded in. My imagination didn't stop with the preacher either. When we stood to sing "Blest Be the Tie That Binds," my addled brain stripped robes from every man in the choir, all the way from the chubby, bald one on the end to the red-headed tenor with a jiggling Adam's apple. But most shameful of all was what happened next. Looking for something to calm my wildness, I turned my eyes upward to the stained-glass window at the front of the church. There, all brightly-colored and thin as a sparrow, was Jesus stretched out on a cross. When I first looked, a piece of cloth covered his privates, but then my dirty mind started working again. Oh, sweet Jesus, he was nailed there just naked as a jay bird. Lord, help my filthy soul, I said to myself. I had to do something, so when preacher called for sinners to come forward, I was the first one in the aisle.

"Bless you, Sister Lizzie," Preacher said. I saw beads of sweat on his upper lip. I remember how Ed used to sweat like that when.... "Preacher," I shouted out, "I've got sins to confess."

Preacher bent close and whispered, "God loves you, Sister Lizzie. Unburden your heart."

"When I was sitting back in the pew," I said, "I couldn't even listen to your sermon cause I kept imagining what you'd look like with your clothes off." Preacher's face turned red as a valentine. I kept talking. "Even worse," I said, trying to find suitable words.

"Yes, Sister Lizzie," he urged, his eyes filled with compassion.

I glanced back at the stained-glass window, the one with Jesus on it. Thank the Lord it was covered with the cloth once again. I knew then that I would never be able to confess to a preacher what I had imagined. It was just too sinful. So, right there in that house of God I lied. It just tumbled out naturally, almost as if it were meant to be said. "Preacher," I said, "I've been tempted to dip snuff."

Preacher looked puzzled. He stammered. Then he told me that he guessed there were worse sins. Finally, clearing his throat, he had the congregation bow for final prayer.

It was strange that at a time like that—the most shameful moment in all my life—I would think of snuff. Even after I got home that night I couldn't get it off my mind. I remembered how Mama had sat dipping, that contented cow look on in her eyes. Fact is, I recollected, she didn't even start the habit until after Daddy had his accident down at the sawmill. I wondered.

The very next day, while shopping at the Winn-Dixie, I picked me up a tin of Tube Rose. Soon as I got home, I stuck a pinch in my mouth just the way Mama used to do. It didn't taste half as bad as I'd feared. The bitterness cleared my sinuses and kept my mind off other things.

Now I ain't claiming that Tube Rose can replace Ed. No snuff can do that. Plenty times, I sit here rocking, remembering how smooth Ed's skin felt against mine. No sir, there ain't no substitute for a man. But snuff—well, it's a comfort.

Lyn Cowan, Miss Vera Barlow

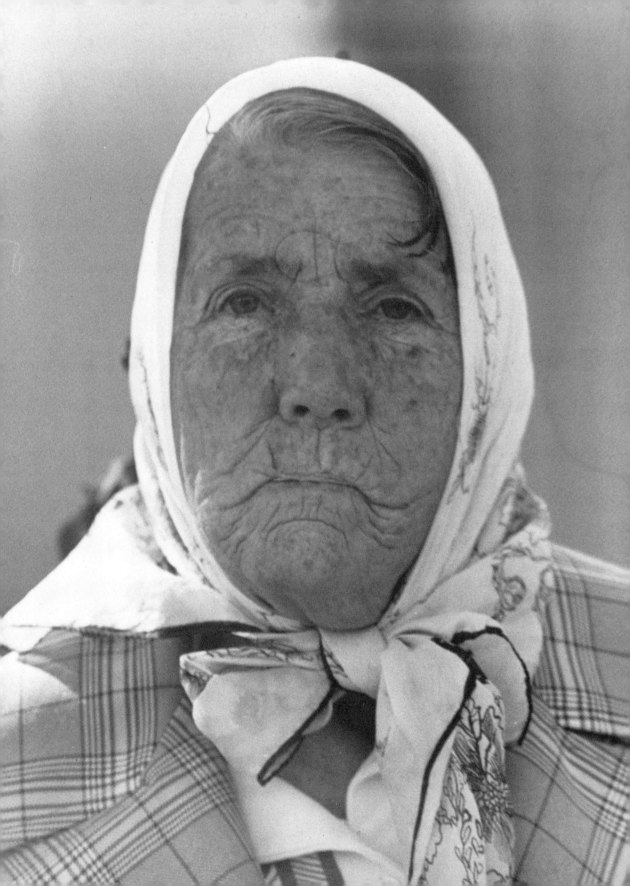

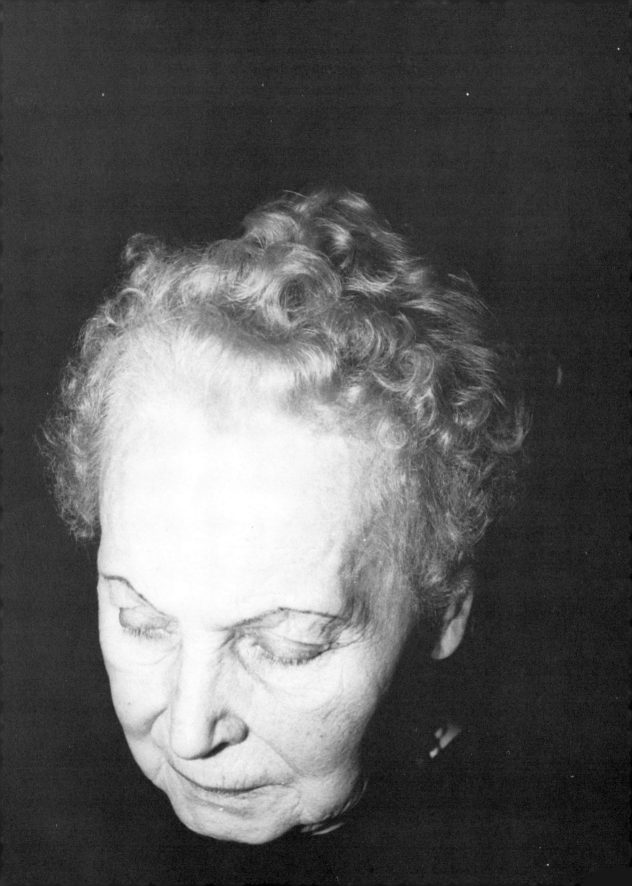

Survived by His Wife

Margaret Flanagan

Eyes swollen she lay in their bed —
head covered, legs drawn up,
cold though her forehead was damp —
who had warmed herself on his warm flesh.

Now his absence was a constant companion:
his hairbrushes, his keys,
his clothes still smelling of him
in his closet, covered, like museum artifacts.

She shuddered, remembering the shoes he wore
were still beneath the bed
exactly as he left them,
as if covered by a glass case.

All of the things he had handled,
used, inhabited, and finally left
were covered or lying about
like the frames of stolen paintings left behind.

Lori Burkhalter, Face of Fern

Making the Wine
Marisa Labozzetta

Angelo is in the bathroom now, shaving. I can hear him singing "Gli Stornelli," belting out the same stanza over and over again in his deep robust voice just the way he used to back in Italy. It is the only song he ever bothered to learn at all. Soon he will come into the kitchen for his orange and cup of black coffee. Peeling the rind in a circular fashion as though he were carving one of his fine pieces of wood, he'll say, "Caterina, take some; it's good for you," and hold out a slice with the same hand that is still gripping the sharp paring knife.

I try to steady my hand as I lift the cup of coffee to my lips. Steady. Steady. Ah! I have spilled some on the table and Sophie must help me put the cup down. She wipes the table—her clean table. Now, Tom, Sophie's husband, has that look on his face as he sits across from me. He always looks like that when I spill something, or eat with my hands, or—almost all the time. I want to say to him, wait, you have no idea what it's like. You can't walk, you can't work, you can hardly think. But all I can manage are the same words each time, "I'm sorry." He gets up and walks out of the room.

Angelo is putting on his lumber jacket and going out to the garden. I tell him that I would go with him but my legs are very swollen. I have not been to the garden in years. Angelo goes religiously every day. He plants and weeds and keeps the rows of tomatoes, beans, eggplant and squash neat like church pews. Then, at the end of the season, we can five hundred jars of tomatoes for Sunday gravy. Angelo has to have his pasta on Sunday. He loves to wake up to the aroma of his tomatoes seasoned with sweet *basilico* simmering for hours in the thick red sauce.

When the children were young, they used to come home from church and dip chunks of thick-crusted bread in the bubbling hot gravy. "It's not done yet!" I warned them, but they loved it anyway. Then, it was the grandchildren. They would walk over on Sunday mornings after church and do the same.

I never went to church. I wish I had. I made sure the children went, though. Children need religion, I used to think; but now I see it is old people who need it. Sophie won't take me. She says the Mass is too long and I will have to go to the bathroom. Once she brought the priest here to hear my confession. It was the third time I had gone to confession in my life. The first time was my First Holy Communion in Italy, all of us dressed like little brides. The second was fifty years later. I don't know what possessed me, but I wanted to go. Angelo laughed at me. He said I had nothing to confess. He said priests did not deserve to hear anyone's sins. When I came home, I told Angelo all about it, how I said it had been fifty years since my last confession. He called me a fool and, cursing, left the room.

Angelo taught me everything about life. I married him when I was almost sixteen; I didn't know anything. I didn't want to marry him but my parents made me. He was really very kind to me. With so much blond hair, blue eyes and a Roman nose, my sisters thought he was wonderful. I thought he was too short. I didn't like any men; all I wanted to do was sit in a corner of the kitchen and read books. When Angelo came calling, I would pretend I was tired and go to bed. But he was so gentle, he took me to America and taught me everything. He told me there were diseases that people could get from making love. He knew because one of his *paisanos* had gotten sick from a town whore. She had wanted Angelo to make love with her but he wouldn't. He is so smart, Angelo.

Angelo is always hugging me and every night he wants to have a love affair with me. I don't like it so much. I'm tired at night and the heaviness of his body on my chest is suffocating. Sometimes I think he will crush my lungs. And it is messy; he soils my clean sheets. Angelo is disappointed but I just don't like it. But there was one time. I don't like to think about it. Angelo was so angry. Father Cioffi had come to visit; Angelo was at the barber's. The baby was only six months old then, and Father Cioffi kept bouncing him onto our bed, then lifting him high into the air and down onto the bed again. When Angelo saw the rumpled bedspread and the priest's black shirt pulled partly out of his black pants, he was furious. He ordered him to leave without an explanation; then he called me *putana,* "whore," he said. I cried and explained that nothing had happened but he left the apartment cursing. I was already in bed when he came back. He undressed quickly and began stroking my hair. When he climbed on top of me and pulled up my nightgown, I didn't mind; I was thinking of Father Cioffi, what it would be like, his tall strong body, his curly black hair.

I think I will wash the dishes for Sophie. I want to but where is the soap? I know it's here on the sink. Is this it? No. That's Sophie's china ashtray. Now she's grabbing it out of my hands. "I only wanted to wash the dishes," I tell her. "Just sit down, Mamma," she says, "just sit down."

Angelo will be coming in for lunch soon. He will want a plate of escarole, a piece of fresh Italian bread and a large glass of red wine. I hope Sophie has remembered to fill the small bottle with wine from the basement. "How is the garden?" I ask him, as he comes in the door. "It will be a good garden this year, Boss." Boss. He has called me Boss forever. I do tell him what to do often. Maybe sometimes too much. But he needs it; he is too easygoing. There are always things to be done. You must work. Angelo likes to drink wine and laugh with people. His laugh is high pitched, almost hysterical. He does everything totally. I don't laugh too much. I have to work. Work is important. You can't have anything without working. Do you think we would have this land if I had not saved all our money? Oh, Angelo worked too, six sometimes seven days a week in the lumber yard, but he never made much money. Every night, he came home with splinters and he and Sophie would sit by the coal stove under the kitchen light. Sophie would take a sewing needle she had sterilized with the flame of a match and poke at his callused hand while he screamed. He is very strong, Angelo; but if he is hurt, he cries out a lot just like a baby. Like when he has attacks of the gout and screams when I walk into the room because vibrations make the sheet touch his foot. I stay awake all those nights. I want to sleep on the couch, to get some rest; I have to work the next day. But Angelo will not let me. He says I have to sleep with him in his bed every night. I am his wife.

I think I will put some coffee on for Angelo. Just turn on the gas. There. It will be done soon.

"Mamma, what are you doing!"

"What are *you* doing?" Damn you, Sophie! You are always taking things away from me. Damn you! I'll slap you! Again! Again!

"This is an electric coffeepot, Mamma. You've ruined it!"

But I never use an electric coffeepot. Angelo likes me to use the drip maker for his espresso. I keep it warm over the flame just before I pour it into his favorite demitasse. Then, he puts in a few drops of *anisetta* and a twist of lemon rind. I never use an electric pot. And that man sitting across the kitchen table keeps staring at me with that look again.

"Sophie, who is that man?"

"It's Tom, Mamma."

"Why don't you let go of my hand? Sophie, you're hurting my hand!"

I must turn on the radio now. After lunch, Angelo likes to listen to the news and then the stock market report. We don't own many stocks, just a few of AT&T, but Angelo likes to know what's going on. I don't understand it very much. Still, if it weren't for me, Angelo would never have been able to buy those stocks. I work hard, day after day, in the machine shop sewing clothes. Even though Angelo is retired, I still work, and he drives me to the machine shop in town every morning and picks me up each evening. I look out of the fourth story window of the factory and see him sitting in the old black Dodge. He is always there twenty minutes before quitting time. He is never late.

But Angelo spends too much money. Like the time he bought a sixty dollar typewriter for Sophie during the Depression, and in cash! He could not turn away the young salesman standing in the doorway of our apartment. Or the time he bought me the diamond brooch for our fiftieth wedding anniversary. I was angry. He should not have ordered a custom-made brooch from Italy. I yelled at him for spending so much money. And I showed him. I never wore it until the day he died; since then, I have never taken it off.

Angelo is going outside now to work on the trellis he is building for my roses. He knows how much I love flowers. "Be careful," I tell him.

"Don't worry, Boss," he laughs.

"And the grape arbor, don't forget to fix the grape arbor!"

Every year Angelo and I make gallons and gallons of wine. The last time we made the wine it happened. I knew I shouldn't have made it; I felt the pressure mounting in my chest; it was getting hard to breathe. But we had to make the wine. If we didn't, the grapes would go bad. All that time and money would be wasted. We had to make the wine; and we did. And it happened. My heart. I remember the first time I opened my eyes after the attack. Angelo was standing over my hospital bed like a frightened schoolboy on his first day of class. Suddenly, he threw himself across my still body and wept even harder than when the baby died, harder than I had ever seen him before. I took his hand in mine and held it as tightly as I could. "Don't cry, Angelo," I said, "I made it. Didn't I?" He nodded. "I made the wine, Angelo. I made it."

Angelo loves living here in the country. It reminds him of our *paese* in the mountains of Rome. Thanks to me, we were able to save the money to buy it. I used to cook cheap meals and sew the children's clothes so we could save. And little by little, we saved enough to buy a few acres, then a few more. And we never owed anybody—nobody. Angelo is different here with the grand-children. In the city he was mean and strict with our children. He was afraid for them—this new country with all of its freedom. There were so many things to get in trouble with—gangsters, cars, subways. If the children were not home on time, he would go out looking for them; and then, when he got them home, he would send them from one side of the kitchen to the other with a single slap. But here in the country he plays with the children, chasing them around the farm with his belt folded in half and snapping it, pretending he will catch their fingers in it if they dare to stick them in. But we are not in the country anymore, are we? And work? I can barely lift myself from this chair which has become a part of me, an extension of myself.

"I have to go to the bathroom again," I tell Sophie.
"It's too late, Mamma. Look what you've done!"
I don't remember doing it. One minute I had to go to the bathroom and the next minute I called Sophie. Maybe it wasn't the next minute. Maybe it was a long time after. Is that possible? I keep looking at Sophie, waiting for her to tell me if it was a long time after.
It is almost four o'clock. I have to turn on the television because Angelo will be in soon and he will want to watch our

story. This and wrestling are the only programs he loves. When he watches wrestling, he screams and laughs as though he were right there in the audience. Oh, and "Gunsmoke," he loves to watch "Gunsmoke." But our story is his favorite. It's on every day and is about a nice girl named Nicole. Nicole has a lot of problems. Right now she is pregnant but can't find the father of the baby, who really loves her, but doesn't know she is pregnant. Every afternoon, we watch to see what Nicole will do. I hope Sophie is making stuffed peppers and sausage for dinner. Angelo likes to eat stuffed peppers and sausage on Monday nights. I think I smell sausage.

After dinner, Sophie gives me a bath. I wish I could bathe myself, but I can't seem to remember what to do. I get into the tub and I am fine. I go for the soap and I get confused. I get so confused. Then my head begins to hurt and I am dizzy. I'm afraid I will fall. But I'm sitting. My head hurts so much.

"Sophie, it hurts."

"What hurts, Mamma?"

"I don't know."

I always feel good after my bath, but I never want to take one. Sophie tells me it's good for me, but I'm afraid. Tom tells me I'm dirty and smell. I never know what will happen to me there in all that water. I don't care if I smell; I'm afraid.

Yesterday, or maybe it was last week, Sophie took me to a nursing home. It wasn't really a nursing home but something better. The floors were very shiny and it smelled like a hospital. There were groups of people sitting in wheel chairs singing old songs. They looked so young; I like to sing.

We sat in an office and a man behind a desk asked me a lot of questions. I knew I had five children, but I couldn't remember any of their names, just Sophie's. I couldn't remember one other name.

"She knows the words to old songs," Sophie said right away.

"Fine, then, let's hear one," the man said.

So I started singing "Ramona," but when I looked at Sophie, she was crying, without a sound, just tears streaming down her face. Don't cry, Sophie, I can remember the words. Don't worry, I thought, I know the words.

Then, a funny thing happened. The man said "no" to Sophie; he said I didn't qualify. And Sophie helped me out, and she was smiling.

Tomorrow is the anniversary of Angelo's death, and I want Sophie to take me to church to the Mass they will say for him. Angelo never went to church after the time with Father Cioffi, but they will say a Mass for him anyway. I didn't tell the priest he never went to church. He should have gone; we both should have gone.

I sleep with Angelo tonight as I have for all these years. He snores loudly and rhythmically to the noisy ticking of the alarm clock on the night table. I have never known any other man in this way except him. I want to have a love affair with you tonight, Angelo. What? No, I cannot promise I will like it, but I won't complain. Please, can we have a love affair tonight?

Come to Me

Sue Saniel Elkind

Come to me looking
as you did 50 years ago
arms outstretched
and I will be waiting
virgin again
in white that changes
to splashes of roses
as we lie together
Come to me smiling again
with your mortar and pestle
and vitamin pills
because I am given to colds
and coughs that wrack us both
Oh come to me again
and I will be there
waiting with withered hands
gnarled fingers
that will leave their marks
of passion on your back.

Lori Burkhalter, Lou and Ruth

Two Willow Chairs
Jess Wells

This is a lesbian portrait, I tell my friends, pointing at the photo in a thick silver frame on my desk, but they don't understand. To them, it's just a snapshot of two empty chairs and they cock their heads at me, wondering why the photo has a place of honor and the chairs are the subject of such elaborate plans.

I took the picture when I was seventeen, which made the chairs brand new, my mother's sister Ruth and her lover Florence in their fifties and their relationship in its fifteenth year. Flo's chair is made of boughs of willow, twisted into locking half moons, a rugged chair that somehow looks like filigree. Next to it on their lawn, a secluded, overgrown stretch of grass and overhanging vines, was Ruth's chair, a simpler one with a broad seat and armrests that gape like a hug. All around the chairs are flowerbeds usually gone to seed and grass that was never "properly cut," my stepfather would growl in the car on the way home from visits, grass thick like fur that Flo would wiggle her toes in, digging into the peat until her feet were black and she would hide them inside their slippers again.

The year of this snapshot, Aunt Florence was "struck with spring" as she used to say to me. We arrived on the Fourth of July to find blooming peonies and iris and marigold ("always marigolds against the snails" she would whisper to me, as if imparting the wisdom of womanhood). Florence and my mother wandered the garden, pointing at stalks and talking potting soil, promising cuttings to each other and examining the grape vines up the trellis, while Ruth and my stepfather faced each other silently, she slumped in the willow chair like a crestfallen rag doll and he sitting rigid, twisted sideways on the plastic webbing of a broken chrome chair. I wandered the yard alone with the garden hose. After ten minutes of listening to the women's voices but not hearing anything, Ruth got up and slouched into the house to start bringing out the beers, calling to the man in an overly loud voice, "So, Dick" (everyone else called him Richard), "how's business?"

Talking commerce was a great diversion for him, and my mother was already occupied with explaining her begonias, which left me to be the only one in the place grappling with the realization that this lesbian child was being deposited for the summer with the family's lesbian aunts because a new stepfather, two brothers and a male cat were more than I could possibly stand. It was the first of many such summers, visits that after a few years turned into summers with autumns and then special Christmases and soon all important holidays and all important matters of any kind. That first summer, nervously pacing the backyard, I knew it would develop into this and when my parents finally left, Ruth and Florence and I stared at each other with wonderment. They'd never had a family before and all of a sudden they had a daughter, full-grown and up in their face feeling awkward. Since my mother was straight, there was something I could dismiss about her, but here were these two, with the weight of maturity *and* the righteousness of twenty years of lesbian lifestyle behind them. Now *that's* what I considered authority.

Aunt Ruth breathed a sigh of relief after the car had pulled out of the drive. Florence let some of her gaiety drop but turned to me, ready to fulfill her last social obligation of the day.

"Beetle," as she called me since I was a baby with big eyes. "Welcome." There was so much hesitancy in her voice, fear almost, as if this child, who did not really know about being a lesbian, were looking at a lesbian who did not really know about being in a family. I dropped the garden hose and wiped my hands on my pants, trying to smooth my carrot-red hair that was frizzy in six different directions, as Florence strode over and gathered me in her arms.

"I don't know about these chairs," Ruth said, getting up and yanking one out of the grass. "Let's take them back by the trellis," she said to me, "Florence's favorite spot." And we all grabbed chairs, me taking my mother's chrome one since it was known to all but Richard that his was the only broken chair in the place. We settled into the afternoon, our conversation picking up pace, while Florence shuttled lemonade and beers. That's when I got my first photo of the chairs.

Ruth was sitting sideways, her leg slung over the arm of the chair, head thrown back, her whole big body lit by a streak of afternoon sun. Florence was struck by spring only in selected places and the back of the yard was not one of them: the grape vines behind Ruth's head dangled low and free, the grass crept up around her chair even though it was early in the season.

We had become very quiet for a moment and Ruth turned in her chair to talk privately to Florence. My camera caught her in mid-sentence, her mouth open, hand reaching for her lover's knee, her eyes still not aware that Aunt Flo was in the house and that she and I were alone, her face showing all the tenderness and history and trust in her femme as she turned to ask "Wren, what was the name of that..."

Ruth looked back at me. "I wish you'd quit with that camera," she growled weakly as I laid the photo on the tops of the tall grass to develop, already sensing that I had exposed her. And in a way, she was right. Until then, I had used this camera as a form of self-defense, silently proving to my brothers how stupid they looked, threatening to catch them in the act, snapping photos of my mother as if trying to prove to myself that she wasn't just a phantom woman. But this day, this photo of Ruth and the empty willow chair was the first photo I had ever taken in an attempt to preserve something beautiful.

I handed the photo to Florence first, as she returned with two beers and a lemonade. She stared at it a long time, seeing the look on Ruth's face.

"Oh God, Wren, get rid of that! I look like a jerk," Ruth protested, but Florence held the photo to her.

"You look wonderful. Besides, I want a photo of my chairs. Here Beetle, take a picture of the chairs for me. Rudy, get up. God, I wish the garden looked better."

Florence kept the two photos in her jewelry box for years. The two willow chairs stayed in their places in the back of the yard and whenever I would visit (on leave from the Army, or home from another city) we would first convene at the chairs, even during the winter, when we would huddle in big coats and share important news like a ritual before rushing inside for the evening.

Years later, when Florence gave the photos to me, there was one taken of myself and Flo sitting on a porch step, our pant legs rolled up from gathering mussels in the tidepools. Florence is gesturing to me, her arms in the shape of a bowl.

"Now look, honey," she said, "don't give up. Love is just a matter of the right recipe: a cup and a half of infatuation, a pinch of matching class status, two tablespoons of compatible politics and three generous cups of good sex. Mix. Sprinkle liberally with the ability to communicate and fold into a well-greased and floured apartment. You bake it for at least six months without slamming the door and pray you have love in the morning. And it works—when you've got the right ingredients."

Of course their relationship was a serious one, so I have photos of times when the recipe wasn't quite right with the two of them, either. In the package with the other photos is a black and white from the '50s of Florence in a wool suit and a hat with a veil standing at the rail of an ocean liner. She and Ruth put all the money they had into a ticket for her to go to Europe and even though it was the most incredible trip she'd ever taken she looks miserable in the picture. The veil is down over her face, almost to her lips that are thick with lipstick and she's wearing kidskin gloves but not waving. She looks very tight and cold to me in this picture but they hung it in their house for years: Ruth liked how smart Flo looked but Aunt Florence would stand in front of it, holding my hand (even though I was home on leave for the third and last year) and say, "Beetle, I keep it because it reminds me of when I was less frightened of running and being alone than of staying and loving." She turned to me, one hand on her hip. "Now isn't that incredible, to think that it's less scary to have a lousy relationship than a good one? That intimacy is more terrifying than loneliness. God, the world is so crazy, Beetle. It's like saying garbage is more delectable than food." Well, I stood in front of that photo with her, looking up at her glowing face, then back at the picture of that sunken young thing and it seemed her face now wasn't wrinkled by age, just stretched from being so open. I thought about my latest crush in the barracks and how good Florence's choice seems to have been (after all, here was the home and the warmth and Ruth lounging on the sofa throwing cashews to the dog), but I looked back at that picture, those eyes big and scared and I knew that's where I was, a veil over *my* face. I turned from my aunt and thought, *Oh Jesus, somebody send me a ticket and point me towards the ocean.*

Ruth kept the photo at her side of the bed, as if to remind herself of how far Florence had run and how close she now lived.

On Florence's side of the bed was a photo taken the summer after she returned. The two are in funny swimsuits with pointed bras, Ruth sleeping in Florence's arms. Flo is bending to kiss her on the neck and years later, she related to me that, lying in the sand with her lover in her arms, Florence could feel the years passing. She could feel Ruth getting older even though she was in her thirties, feel her getting heavier through middle age, belly growing across her hips, feel her shift in her sleep from an injury to her shoulder that she didn't have yet, saw the scars she would have in the future, Ruth getting smaller and more frail as she aged, wrinkling into buttery skin. And all the time, holding Ruth encircled in her arms, Florence knew that this would be the progress of her world, that this was her future and her life, that this woman between her arms was her home.

Of course Flo had pictures of her Mom and Dad, who have been dead for nearly two decades now, and the family at picnics, Ruth playing horseshoes on her sixtieth birthday and pictures of me when I was a kid with teeth missing, though we won't go into that. There's another lesbian portrait in this stack from Flo — it's a picture of a dog.

Clarise was the spaniel that Florence had when she was lovers with the woman before Ruth (which is how she was always referred to, she never had a name) and Flo kept the photo on top of the television for years after she had left the woman and the dog. The little thing was sitting attentively on the beach, clumps of dirt hanging on its paws. It was the first dog Florence had ever learned to love and every year, with a faraway look in her eyes, Flo would ramble on about how special and psychic and beautiful and protective it was. It was everything a dog should be. Just a few years ago, Ruth, sick and lying on the couch, threw off the afghan and snatched the photo off the TV.

"For Godsake Florence, it's over, and it's OK that it's over," she shouted, starting to cough. "The dog wasn't the only thing good and the woman wasn't the only thing bad. Now com'on."

Florence went into the back yard and sat in her willow chair. It was her seventieth birthday and she should have a jacket, I thought.

"Stay here, Beetle," Ruth said.

"I don't see why you're jealous of a dog, Rudy. For

Christsake, it was years ago."

"I'm not jealous. Florence doesn't know what to do with all those years spent with that woman and so she puts them here," she said, tapping the glass frame. "When you're consumed with bitterness, where do you put all the good times? The dog. The only reason I'm even saying it is because she knows it herself. A couple of months ago, we went to Bolinas, remember...?"

"Where we used to gather mussels?"

"Right. Well, Wren thought the air would make me feel better or something, but who should come trotting up but the spitting image of that dog. Splatters mud all over Wren's newspaper, knocks the damn iced tea into the potato chips and rolls over to stick up her tits. I mean it. Well, it finally dawns on Wrenny, Goddamn, maybe that Clarise was just a fucking dog, too."

Now I have the photo. I keep it with a bunch of others Florence gave me in a white, unmarked envelope. These are the painful pictures, the ones that bring floods of heat to your face, pictures you look at and smell perfume. There's a picture of Florence pointing at the flowerbeds with her cane, trying to get *me* to be struck with spring and do some planting while I waited for Ruth to get well. Then there's Ruth lying on the couch covered with the afghan, looking tiny and angry, and after she died, a photo of Florence looking remarkably like her picture in the hat with the veil. Florence never went back to the chairs after Ruth died, never went into the back of the yard, only stared at it from the kitchen window, stricken now that Ruth, love, hope and future were dead and decaying, confused by the sight of the grass and the flowers blooming, as if life were threatening to overtake her when she knew it was death that was the encroacher. The grape vines grew lower, entwining with the boughs of the willow chairs, as if threatening to scoop them into a cluster and throw them up to the sun to ripen, while the grass underneath fought to drown the chairs in green. I took a picture of the chairs last year in this condition but I conveniently lost it. I do have a snap of me, fifteen pounds thinner from not sleeping while Florence lay dying and one of my Mom at Flo's wake, crying like she couldn't at Ruth's. Maybe someday I could frame them and hang them and still be able to walk through the room, but I doubt it. Right now all I can manage is that first snap of the two empty chairs. My friends don't understand it. Nor do they understand why I'm borrowing a truck and calling around for a hacksaw.

"I have to save the chairs," I tell them, slamming down the phone on my mother and dashing for my jacket. The house has been sold, finally, my mother tells me and the new owners are sure to throw Wren and Rudy's chairs into the dump—if there's anything left of them. They were nearly part of the grape-vine forest last year when Florence died. First thing in the morning I'll cut the chairs away from the underbrush and drive them to a field near Bolinas where they can sit together and watch the unruly grass grow up around them again, maybe this time forever.

Planting

Cinda Thompson

Two
Old people work
Side by side
She wears a hat
The old man boasts
No hair at all
She moves
And he kneels
He digs
And she nods while
He speaks
To the seed
She ardently covers
Row by row
They rise and bend
Over their garden
On earth
Sunflowers will bloom
Toward
Late summer

Maybe at Eighty?

S. Minanel

They say wisdom comes as you age—
Now I'm in a real jam—
at sixty I should be a sage—
look what a fool I am!

Endurance

Fran Portley

We women who have lived
through many winters
are sisters to mountain flowers
found in rocky crevices
high in the Alps.

Hardened by wind and snow
we endure cold
absorb brief sun
reach long roots
to meager sustenance
lift bright blossoms to empty air.

Becoming Sixty

Ruth Harriet Jacobs

There were terror and anger
at coming into sixty.
Would I give birth
only to my old age?

Now near sixty-one
I count the gifts
that sixty gave.

A book flowed from my life
to those who needed it
and love flowed back to me.

In a yard that had seemed full
space for another garden appeared.
I took my aloneness to Quaker meeting
and my outstretched palms were filled.

I walked further along the beach
swam longer in more sacred places
danced the spiral dance
reclaimed daisies for women
in my ritual for a precious friend
and received poet's wine
from a new friend who came
in the evening of my need.

Social Security
Barbara Bolz

She knows a cashier who
blushes and lets her use
food stamps to buy tulip
bulbs and rose bushes.

We smile each morning as I
pass her—her hand always
married to some stick
or hoe, or rake.

One morning I shout,
"I'm not skinny like
you so I've gotta run
two miles each day."

She begs me closer, whispers
to my flesh, "All you need,
honey, is to be on welfare
and love roses."

Lori Burkhalter, Mrs. Hufford

Litany for a Neighbor

Ellin Carter

Jubilate Dea

Because you wear a sunbonnet in your garden
      and wash doilies and dry them on
      newspapers on the carpet, and all
      your African violets bloom.

Because you live on the next street, not
      next door, and you do not even imply
      a comment on the state of my yard.

Because you took in my cat Mushroom when
      he left home, repelled by our new
      kitten, and succored him during
      a blizzard.

      (And even though he will never come
      home, for so long as you both may live,
      I still forgive you.)

Because, though they pass through an alley
      of Doberman pinschers, all the cats
      of the neighborhood congregate in
      your grape arbor, where they rise up
      and worship you.

The Wildcat

Catherine Boyd

The Schraders, who live up the street, saw it first. They heard their garbage can tip over and when they turned on their floodlights it was tearing open green Hefty bags and devouring scraps. It lifted its small fierce head and screeched a warning to stay back — and in two bounds the wildcat was gone.

For a while, there were daily reports. The Keifer's trash can, lodged in a frame of four-by-four posts, had its rubber-clamped lid forced off; its booty was plundered. The Gabrielsons heard crying one night but aren't sure which direction the sounds came from. Todd Henny, coming home late from a planning commission meeting, passed the junipers on his long driveway and caught the reflection of the wildcat's steely eyes as it disappeared into the night.

Todd is a bachelor and a keeper of fish. He had left a window open that night and he found its screen shredded. On his living room floor was a mess of broken glass, water, orange and turquoise gravel and the remains of a half-eaten pacu.

After this a trap was set in Todd's back yard because he doesn't have any children who might step on it. The Stewarts and the Keifers put poison in their trash cans, and the Animal Control sent out a notice instructing us to call immediately if we ever saw it, no matter the time, day or night.

I often dream of the wildcat. Usually I dream I come upon it by accident in the yard, or while in the pantry or going somewhere in the car. One time, in my dream, I was awakened by its calling. It was early morning, the light was soft, the air pure, the day clear and inviting in a way I had completely forgotten a day can be. I stumbled from bed and down the stairs. The wildcat was on the screened porch at the back of the house. It was not so small and it gave me a quick look of recognition — and then it took off.

I swung open the screen door and followed as fast as I could. The wildcat scrambled over the fence, and it wasn't until I was halfway over that I remembered I am seventy-nine years old and can no longer scale six-foot walls. Still, I kept looking over the fence. I saw the wildcat dart playfully back and forth through a field of oats and dandelions, an endless field that wasn't there when I woke, feeling fit and happy, put my robe on and went out to the back yard.

The presence of the wildcat in the neighborhood has brought a change to my routine. In the morning, after I've had breakfast, watched the "Today" show and cleaned the kitchen, I turn everything off and lie on the couch in the living room with my eyes closed. I search my mind for dreams, or fragments of dreams, I may have had about the wildcat. If I find one I recreate it a few times before going on with my day.

The mail comes at about ten-thirty. It's mostly junk, solicitations for cruises or clubs or hearing aids, or publications that will tell you how best to care for your health and organize your finances. But there are often letters, too, and the magazines my late husband, David, and I read together at night for almost fifty years.

After lunch I check the local paper. I know if anything ever happened to the wildcat, it would be in the newspaper. There used to sometimes be an article, in the middle pages, a few lines describing the latest pilferage or fright the wildcat had caused, though for more than a month there has been nothing.

Every afternoon I drive a little farther to reach a pet shop I haven't used yet. I pretend to not be looking only for six pacu. I remember to not talk too much. I pay with cash, never a check or the Master Charge. When I get home I put the fish in a bucket in the potting shed. I lock the shed door.

Sometimes I go to afternoon teas, or dinner parties, and these times with friends are pleasant diversions from my routine. But I keep my nights to myself by claiming to retire at nine o'clock. I don't. As much as anything I enjoy the late hours at my desk in the study, where I keep up a steady correspondence with my three children, and their children.

When I'm sure the lights at the Worbys' house have been extinguished for the night, I put on my robe and walk out to the potting shed, get the bucket and carry it to the flower bed near the back fence. I set it down. Then I go back inside, slide open a window to the living room, stretch out on the couch and begin reading from whatever book I'll bring to bed that night.

When I hear the splashing sounds I slip a marker in the book, look up to the ceiling and sigh. I feel released. Content. Pleased. Although the splashing lasts but a few minutes, it's an integral part of my routine, a way of almost formally declaring an end to another day.

A sudden silence tells me it's finished. I go out to the back fence again. I pour the water out of the bucket, onto the flower bed. I whisper to my friend, "You'll always be safe with me."

Out of the Lion's Belly
Carole L. Glickfeld

She maintained that she'd had a marvelous sabbatical in Kenya, even in the face of those who were saying it had unhinged her and were calling for her dismissal from Lincoln Junior High School, where she taught art. These facts were undisputed: That before her year in Kenya, she had been a model teacher; she had been punctual, never arriving late to school nor failing to turn in her lesson plans in a timely fashion; she had graded her pupils' papers promptly and had been prompt for meetings with parents; she had promoted and achieved order, using only her softly modulated tones, never the shrill rage or the nasal sarcasm that were the modus operandi of the other teachers attempting to hold twelve-year-olds in check.

When the matter came to court, almost two years later, she again said, this time to the jury, looking past the shoulder of the interrogating attorney for the school district, that the sabbatical had been the highlight of her years, second only to the many hours she'd spent teaching Lincoln's junior high school pupils art, or, as she developed her notion, "those elements of art that would in some lingering way enhance and enlarge the vision of what in this life was important. Vision with a capital V."

"And did that year in Africa change your vision, Miss Inwood?" the attorney asked, pronouncing "Africa" as though it were a dark, vermin-infested cellar.

She blinked rapidly, and cocked her head. "But of course it did."

"In what way?"

"Why, in every way."

"Would you elaborate on that, Miss Inwood?"

She did or she didn't, according to your perspective. The paper had it that her lengthy anecdote was interrupted by the judge, who asked her to "get to the point."

Her anecdote centered on a fluffy lion cub, "a ball of the palest angora," rolling around on its back a few feet from its watchful mother, a few yards from a hotel veranda where Miss Inwood had sat drinking tea out of a fine china cup. "Imagine the moonlight, a platinum moon, a three-quarters moon, oblong, you know, and ever so slightly askew, a *trompe l'oeil*, of course. The lions were the color of the moon, almost without hue, luminescent, but later, when I attempted to paint them, I found —"

The key witnesses for the school district included two pupils, their mothers, and the school principal. The attorney referred to the Zweigs as "measuring sticks," because Miss Inwood had been Marilyn Zweig's art teacher both the year before the sabbatical and the year after. The testimony of Elliot Marcus and Mrs. Marcus was said to be of "value" because those witnesses represented pupils and parents "without preconceived expectations of what constituted Miss Inwood's usual behavior." The attorney went on to say, "I submit to you that we will fully detail the defendant's unfitness to teach, the intolerable situation that her behavior created, behavior which, and I state this advisedly, clearly demonstrates that she has gone off the deep end —"

"Objection!" said Miss Inwood's attorney, rising to his feet. "We are not presenting any psychiatric evidence here. Counsel has no expertise —"

"With all due respect," the plaintiff's attorney said, " 'off the deep end' refers to behavior at the most extreme end of the scale, the scale being the range of what we agree is normal, customary, acceptable. As I say, way, way off the scale's very end —"

Miss Inwood was my teacher. Not in a public school, but in

her home. She had long since "retired," she told me, from public school teaching, giving private lessons "to a select few." I'd heard about her from a friend who used to take lessons from her, which she found "disturbing." The nature of the disturbance intrigued me, having less to do with the fine quality of the lessons than Miss Inwood's habits. "She's a trip," my friend said. "Practically buried in her art. It's her whole world, but then she goes off on these peculiar tangents, the same ones all the time."

Since neither single-mindedness nor eccentricity seemed to me faults, I called Miss Inwood. She said I would have to appear for an interview.

"How many samples should I bring?"

"Of your work? None, dear. Just bring yourself. Your best self."

Her house was a small colonial brick with a wrought iron gate enclosing several giant oak trees. My satisfaction at having chosen an art teacher who had taste wavered, however, when she opened her door. Over her blouse and skirt she wore a pink organdy pinafore apron, trimmed with a two-inch white ruffle, red rickrack and appliqued blue and yellow flowers.

"That's interesting!" she said, pointing to my hair. "Does it make you feel off balance?"

I had one of those fashionable asymmetrical cuts, above the ear on one side, below on the other. "Jazzy, rather," I said.

Her glance travelled down my clothes, a Shetland sweater over a buttoned-down shirt and jeans. She nodded and stepped aside to let me in.

"I've been baking. Excuse my apron. I mean, the raffishness of it. My sister-in-law has raffish taste. Isn't that a good word?"

My breathing resumed its normal rhythm.

"Go ahead, talk to me," she said, sitting me down at the kitchen table. "I have to punch this down and then you'll have my full attention." Her manner suggested a lady of a large country mansion, whose grace had a pleasant dottiness that signalled her safe remove from the real world.

"What are you making?" I asked, watching as she pummeled the ball of dough and then slapped it against the cutting board, picking it up and slapping it down again.

"Two whole wheat loaves," she said, looking up at me. Her blue eyes were small, crinkly, deeply set beneath her arched grey brows. She looked as though she were perennially asking a question. "So, you're the conservative type," she said, using her lower lip to direct her breath upwards, blowing away a grey, curly wisp which had fallen onto her forehead. She shaped the dough into another ball, placed it in a bowl which she covered with a linen towel and set in the oven. "Away from drafts," she explained.

"Is your painting also conservative?" she asked, pouring me a cup of tea. She set down a platter of chocolate chip cookies and then poured herself some tea. "Is it?" she repeated.

"I don't think so. Although I haven't been what I'd call experimental."

"If we start our lessons soon, we'll have five months until I go to Hawaii. I always go to Hawaii in February." She paused, clearly expecting me to ask why.

"Not for a vacation?" I said.

"You think not?" Her eyes, beginning to dance, told me I was onto something. But what?

"To paint!" I guessed.

She slapped her hand on the table. "I could tell by the sound of your voice, dear, but I wanted to see you. Really *see* you, capital S, with my own eyes. If I may venture to say so, I think you are seeing me, capital S. So the matter of *whether* you will be my pupil is moot. Have a cookie."

I had been her pupil for a couple of months before she showed me any of her paintings, taking me into her attached garage, which she'd converted into a second studio with skylights. The

paintings stood on the floor, leaning against the walls, and there was one, in progress, on an easel. "I won't let you guess which is which," she said, pointing out to me that her "riotous phase" was over and that she was in a more "subdued" period. Her riotous phase had solely to do with her sabbatical in Africa, it seemed, to which she referred more and more as our intimacy increased.

"Bougainvillea! You've never seen such bougainvillea: rich mauves and reds. And, my dear, the hibiscus, the yellow flowering acacia. The perfumes. Have you ever smelled freesia, fields of it which fairly *intoxicate* you? That was in the Central Province. My African students laughed. Oh did they laugh! Why paint pictures of flowers when you could have them for the plucking, they asked.

"I thought you were there on sabbatical."

"And so I was. From my duties here. I taught in a little village, part of a Teachers' Exchange Program. I couldn't tell you who or what they exchanged for me. Hah! I was there to educate the natives. You can guess the end of that story. They educated me."

Her African paintings were almost magical, both eerie and lush. She painted them by moonlight or by the light of dawn. "My flora and fauna," she said, the way another grey-haired seventy year old woman might have said, "my grandchildren." She knelt by one of them. "Did you ever imagine acacia so verdant?" she asked. "Giraffe so peaceful?" Then, rising, she pointed to another painting of hyena and jackals at sunrise. "Can you guess what they're up to?"

"Having their breakfast?"

"Bones, probably, left over from the catch of lion or cheetah the night before. Scavengers of sorts. I too hate to think of bones going to waste. I always use them to make soup, don't you?" Then, pointing to a painting of fuschia and scarlet flowers lining a dirt road, she said, "Do you think the colors *outré*? They're actually understated from the real thing."

Lori Burkhalter, "I've Traveled the Country"

By contrast, her seascapes were muted, even the ones at sunset. "Salable," she told me. "That's how I get to Hawaii, you see. I paint enough to finance my stay in the artists' colony. Don't you think that's a pretentious phrase? Artists' colony. The actuality is not, I assure you. A remote village in Kona. We live simply. What's expensive are the supplies I bring for everyone, boxes and boxes of chalk and charcoal, hundreds of tubes of paint, and a suitcase of canvases."

As she started out of the garage, I stopped, looking over some of the fauna and flora.

"I won't part with those," she said, possibly sensing that I wanted to acquire one from her riotous period.

"If you change your mind," I said.

After she returned from Hawaii (with many pastels of orchids and anthurium), she began to interject some of her former pupils from public school into her monologues, Marilyn Zweig and Elliot Marcus, in particular. But without so much as a hint that they had testified against her, had helped pound nails, so to speak, in her coffin.

One day, during our tea break, which came with clockwork regularity at two hours into the lesson (after which we would paint for another hour before calling it quits), she told me about the first time she'd laid eyes on Elliot.

"Now you have to imagine this leggy boy, almost thirteen you know, and tall, lanky. Like a flamingo, I thought, when he showed up in a peach-colored shirt on first day of class. He was all arms and legs and folded himself into a chair sized for a normal boy, but too small for him. Folded himself like a bird would, into itself, and I knew that he was the one Mrs. Marcus had called me about.

"I always had mothers calling me, you know, just before the semester began, telling me what artistic geniuses their children were. In case I should fail to recognize them. But this one! Mrs.

Marcus called to say her son had no talent for art. 'None whatsoever,' she insisted. Because he was a mathematical genius, a whiz at algebra and geometry and computers. He gets 'uniformly high grades,' she told me, not so subtly cautioning me against putting any dips in the records, you see. Dippety-do-dah, I wanted to tell her. Actually, I did. But that was later. She had her heart set on getting him into the best college, and didn't want art to stand in her way. In his way. No, I guess I got it right the first time. Oh, I nearly forgot the cookies."

She got up to get them, out of an oddly shaped ceramic cannister, which looked like some of the pottery seconds at the annual arts and crafts show. Possibly she'd fashioned it herself. She'd made the cookies, chocolate chip as always. Sitting down, she turned her limpid blue eyes on me and continued her story.

"She wasn't the most unreasonable mother, but her point of view, well, what can I say? She pretended that it was Elliot who thought art was irrelevant, and saying that to me, well, I might just as well have said to her, mothers are irrelevant. Between you and me, dear, they are. After they've given birth.

"So, she demanded to meet me in a coffee shop on the other side of town, in the freezing cold, the snow a foot high, and it was one of my two precious days off, a Saturday. Except, of course, I had a mountain of papers to grade, and a lesson plan to write. I said I didn't think the meeting was necessary. That Elliot's work would have to speak for itself. I gave her my best advice: 'Tell Elliot effort *is* relevant,' and I rung off.

"I remember that call distinctly, because I was working on a painting when the phone rang. You know how that goes, it rings and you try not to answer it, but you always do. I was trying to capture innocence, the purity of it, in a lion cub, not easy to accomplish. It's not just a cute little kitten after all. We never say, Oh it's just a lion, when it grows up. So I was also trying to capture the inherent quality that commands our respect. I'd been working for months, dabbing at it and dabbing. I was afraid it would get away from me, the longer I was back. After the sabbatical." She smiled at me. "Shall we resume our lesson, dear?"

During the tea break the following week, she showed me the Lincoln Junior High Year Book from twenty years ago, which contained the class picture where thirty students stood solemnly in four rows, wearing white shirts or blouses, their arms hanging down at their sides. Except for Elliot, whose elbows jutted out from his long thin body. Marilyn was in the front row, a petite little thing with dark eyes, reminding me of all the would-be poets in my own junior high graduating class.

When we returned to the kitchen table, Miss Inwood took right up again. "Well, where was I? Elliot Marcus. You wouldn't guess what he turned in for his first assignment. I asked them to use straight lines to divide a blank sheet of paper. In an *interesting* manner. He drew a checkerboard! I gave him a B, not because his checkerboard was interesting, but because his thinking of one was. Hah! And his mother called me to complain. She called the principal. He called me. I called her. *Nous avons fait la ronde!*" She made a circular motion with her fist, as though twirling a streamer.

"Did you change the B?" I asked.

"What do you think?" she said.

Her African paintings were reference points, sometimes used as object lessons. "When I tried to get the light filtering through the leaves of the acacia, I didn't merely dab splotches of zinc white," she said to me once, about a still life I was working on. At other times, they comprised her ode to a Grecian urn: "When I think of a time that was idyllic, this is what I think, you see," she'd say, pointing to a trail of elephants or a single reticulated giraffe. And sometimes she used them as a springboard for other subjects, punctuality, for one.

"So I kept dabbing at this painting, you know. And then came a day when I realized I'd never get it right. I slashed the canvas, jumped on it [she stood up and demonstrated the jump], beat it over a chair [she lifted her arms up and brought them down again and again], until it was bent and cracked in a dozen places. Imagine me, a sedate woman, fifty years old, sobbing and shrieking, rocking back and forth like she'd lost her child. Hah! So I started over. But the semester had begun by then, and I no longer had any daylight to speak of, so I'd set the alarm for sunrise and start in, wearing a robe over my nightie and wool kneesocks. Of course, the time would get away from me and I'd have to run a few stoplights to make it to the schoolhouse on time, or almost on time. Not quite on time for Mr. Reynolds. You'd think the world was coming to an end when you were five minutes late. I offered to stay ten extra minutes after school. You must realize the first half hour merely consists of getting your keys and your mail and cleaning your erasers — all those exceedingly important tasks. But no, Mr. Reynolds preferred to make my time card a *cause célèbre*. I didn't come home in much of a mood to paint, but by next morning, hope dawned again, and there I was, creating more grief."

On my way out the door that day, she clutched my arm. "Noisome, palpable fear oozed out of the school district's administration like vile shades of acrylic, drying before they could be tempered. Don't ever let smallmindedness and pettifoggery cloud your vision. With a capital V." It was then I understood that her public career had come to an unhappy conclusion.

Stopping by the library, I made some inquiries, and found the first of many newspaper clippings on the trial. I obtained a copy of the voluminous court record and read it through in two nights. In the court record, she admits to having thrown blackboard erasers across the room, along with chalk, and even a vase of flowers. A glass vase. "I never hurt anyone," she said, in her defense. "I obtained their attention. That's what I'm paid to do."

On a stifling summer day, she took me up to the attic after our lesson was over. She pointed out some miscellaneous objects, a leather desk blotter, a large rectangular desk clock, an atlas. I guess I had expected to see some African artifacts, but there were none. I almost choked on the dust she blew off a plastic bag containing photographs.

"This is me about your age," she said, handing me a picture of a thirtyish woman, wearing a high pompadour and a print dress with obvious shoulder pads. There were other pictures in the bag, but she didn't show them to me. Her glance fell on a set of small notebooks, then she seemed to change her mind about the wisdom of our being in the attic. Abruptly, she twirled the plastic bag closed, laid it down on a marble-topped end table, and descended the ladder. I followed dutifully, unable to see anything further because she held the flashlight.

"See you next week," she said, cheerfully. "And if I don't, remind me." That was a reference to her use of "see," which was seldom casual. She often admonished me to "really see," "look," "absorb," "digest." The most scathing comment she could make about someone's work was that the artist didn't "see" what he or she was painting. Which usually wasn't my problem, thankfully. My problem was a matter of making others "see" what I saw. That is to say, technique.

I worked on my technique. Oh God, how I worked on my technique! I never wanted to please anyone as much as her. She had a canny knack, though, of knowing when I was trying too hard. The lessons we had drove me to study books on composition.

"Is it Utrillo's *Rue Ravignan* you're trying to repaint? Well, don't waste your time, my dear," she might say gingerly, slicing me to the quick.

At such times I wanted to give up the lessons, because I knew I could never paint well enough. But I couldn't give *her* up. The two were inseparable. While I'd entertained thoughts of a friendship with her apart from our lessons, she put dampers on any effort I made to establish one. She would send me only a perfunctory postcard from Hawaii, never answering the letters I wrote her. When I asked her to my home one evening, she said, "I never go out nights." So I invited her to lunch, but her response was, "I'm not the lunching sort."

One afternoon, we were painting a bowl of flowers she had arranged on a lace-clothed table. She put her brush down and came over to look, as she often did, to encourage me or to redirect my efforts, usually with light humor. This time, she seized my arm. "Marilyn Zweig!" she barked.

I looked up to see her blinking at me, as though I were Marilyn incarnate. She looked back at the painting. Then she took the brush from my hand and smeared some of the fine lines I'd drawn on the lace cloth and petals. If you've never had an art lesson and cannot imagine the visceral effect she had on me, imagine someone deliberately pouring grape juice on your favorite dress or tie.

"Take this out!" she demanded. "Marilyn Zweig was in my class for four semesters. I did everything I could to try to make her understand that most of her work was extraneous. I explained, I lectured, I took the entire class on a trip to the museum for her single benefit. I invited her to my home—a mistake, but we won't go into it now. I showed her the painting that had taken everything out of me.

"And just when I had given up hope, she turned in a term project that was stunning. Free of every superfluity. Later it won third prize in the Arts and Crafts Show, a simple line drawing of a black cat with a piece of colorful yarn." She crinkled her eyes, looking up at me, a signal for me to say something.

"That's wonderful!" I said. "You got through."

She smiled ironically, then walked over to a bookcase in the foyer, slipping a piece of paper out from a book. Handing it to me, she said, "What's that?"

It was an advertisement for a car, drawn against the New York skyline.

Without waiting for me to answer, she said, "It's Marilyn Zweig. And if it's not Marilyn, I'll eat this piece of paper. See what good being a public school teacher is?"

I looked at the drawing. No question but that it was cluttered: every window drawn in, every leaf on the trees. Photo-realism was a style I didn't care for, but because Marilyn chose it, did that make Miss Inwood a failure? Besides, the chance that the ad was actually Marilyn's work was one in a million. The style just wasn't that distinctive.

"But the term paper," I protested.

"I gave it an A plus. And then, when I was congratulating myself no end for my success, she said it was Elliot. He had explained it to her, told her I didn't like paintings that looked like photographs, so she should do something else. He suggested Japanese brushstroke. Do you think I should have learned something from that lesson?" She walked over to the other easel and took up her brush. "See what you can do, dear, with your petals. The less the better."

The trial had produced many exhibits: traffic tickets for speeding and running stop lights, time cards showing Miss Inwood's arrival and departure times, homework papers which contained fat red X's through them or abstruse comments, her appointments calendar (to indicate she'd been aware of meetings she missed or had attended late), and the expense voucher she'd turned in for the outing to the Museum (a seventy-mile train trip each way for thirty students). They'd had to subpoena the painting of the lion cub.

She was declared "unfit to serve as a teacher," although she received back pay for the two months during which (before the trial) she was barred from entering the school. Thus, after twenty-seven years of teaching, she was retired, on a full pension, at the age of fifty-two.

One lovely spring afternoon after our lesson, she came out of the house with me, and walked me to the front gate. "Did I ever tell you what Elliot did for his term project? He called it *Chocolate Chip Cookie: Aerial View.* It was a gargantuan, misshapen thing. Lavender dough with purple chips. I could have given him another B, but from that he would learn nothing." She interrupted herself to ask what makes a chocolate chip cookie good.

"I don't know," I said; "I can only tell you what I like."

She smiled. "I ask that of all my pupils. Usually it's the chips or the nuts, sometimes the chewiness. Elliot's answer was, 'the baker.' I'd asked him the question once when he wanted to know what makes a painting good."

"Then what's your answer?"

"What makes anything good — or bad? The jury, of course. Trite but true. Anyway, I gave Elliot Marcus an A plus. He was a very logical young man, you see. I knew he would ponder it, that it would confound him. Because he had done nothing essentially different from the checkerboard, or the torus, or the Moebius strip he had been turning in all along, and certainly nothing to deserve the grade. His average, by the way, came out B plus, so it hardly signified. Except to Mrs. Marcus. But that's another story. I'll see you next week."

When I arrived at her house the next week, though, she didn't answer the door. I thought of calling the police, but on a hunch, I called the hospital. They asked if I was a relative. When I said yes, they said she had "expired."

She left me her diaries and the painting of the lion cub, the one she called, "Out of the Lion's Belly." One of her last entries explains the title: "They said Jomo Kenyatta wanted to bring his country out of the dark jungle and into the age of modern civilization. Indeed, on Kenya's Day of Independence, he said, 'I've snatched you out of the lion's belly.' To Mr. Kenyatta, and to anyone who may read this hence, I've performed some midwifery of my own, so to speak. I repent my arrogance."

Hurricane

Edna J. Guttag

Winifred, eighty years young
Five foot, two inches tall
Expert on ancient Persia and Egypt
Wanted expertise on hurricanes.
Hurried from the Village to the Jersey Shore
Preparing to interrogate
The Ocean's reaction
To jetting gusts and blasting rain,
Content to sit on the porch
Of the empty hotel
Ready to watch the view,
Arthritically fought the policeman, who
Finally able to evacuate her
Carried Winifred off along with possessions
That were not even hers
To the place where all the other evacuees were.
Afterwards, regretfully, she noted aloud,
"But the Sea now is all quiet and calm."

Oh, That Shoestore Used to Be Mine

Randeane Doolittle Tetu

"Oh, that shoestore used to be mine," Paynter pointed a cane at the green front between a flower store and a bakery. Mrs. Tuttle read the gold lettering, Geo. W. Crayton, Shoes. Paynter said, "Wear triple E myself's how I got started in shoes. Stores just don't carry out-of-the-ordinary sizes. I wouldn't be walking today 'cept for the fact that I decided to buy a shoestore and stock the right sizes."

"How many years?" Mrs. Tuttle asked.

"Ago or selling shoes?"

"Selling shoes."

"Well, eighteen or so I'd guess."

The feel of the weight of the shape of the shoe in her hand, the smell of the leather, the kneeling in front of a stockinged foot, then another, the carpeting, the slanted mirror which showed her up from a long way down, the metal and black foot measure with its sliding parts and smell of metal, the shoehorn in the belt did not breathe out of Paynter and Mrs. Tuttle was surprised. Of all the lives they had sketched for Paynter back at the Manor, shoestore owner had not been one.

Angela said, "She never worked. She was supported. You'll see." And Mrs. Tuttle thought she was right.

"We don't know if she's a Miss or a former Mrs. and now we have three Amandas and will have to call her Paynter for short." They sent Mrs. Tuttle to be her buddy to walk into town. "You have a way about you, now, you know you do." Mrs. Tuttle knew she did. "You just come back and tell us all about her."

"Something nice about knowing there're people walking around in shoes you fit for them and feeling fine and doing all wonderful things because their feet don't hurt," Paynter said. At Woolworth's she bought perfumed talc and walked around the aisles.

"They have almond croissants here," she said at the bakery on the way back. "Wouldn't we like a coffee." No one else was in the bakery, and Mrs. Tuttle sat so she could see the sidewalk. Paynter munched the almond croissant and sipped coffee to last a morning. When Mrs. Tuttle finished her Danish she said, "How long were you married?"

"Was married quite a while. Quite a while. Man by the name of Karl. Karl and I were married quite a while. I used to let him help in the store sometimes, mostly behind the counter. I really knew the customers best. He would get bored."

Mrs. Tuttle made her coffee last and said, "Never before stopped here."

"They make a good croissant. I never was much for baking." Mrs. Tuttle thought, Married to Karl eighteen years. Owned shoestore. "Any children?"

"Children. My, yes. Now one's a musician. Plays in the orchestra, you know. And my son is an artist. He's in New York. Now wouldn't you think they could make up some grandchildren? But, no. Neither of them married and no grandchildren."

Mrs. Tuttle added this and sat back. She was feeling grand. Some of the new ones guarded their privacy, tried to save their personalities, hold onto their former lives, not willing to recognize that they were no longer theirs to save once they entered the Manor. This one though was fine. This one was easy. Paynter would tell things fresh from the world with the blush still on.

When they left the bakery, Paynter said, "You go in and see what you can get for an out-of-the-ordinary shoe. You just see. I have eight more shoes like this in my closet you know, or I would never have given it up."

The flower store on the other side said, PAYNTER'S in the stone block and MILDRED GRAYNOR in gold lettering on the door. Mrs. Tuttle stopped and looked at the shoe store window and at the flower shop under the striped awning. "It says Paynter's for the flowers, Amanda. You sure it was a shoestore you owned?"

"A shoestore? Why, no, my dear. I told Clayton flowers. And for eighteen years it was flowers."

"But I thought you just said that shoestore used to be yours."

Paynter looked off down the street to where the sidewalk petered out and turned into the path that would lead to the Manor. "Shoestore, flower store. I know it wasn't the bakery. I never was good at baking. Mildred Graynor," she added for good measure, "that's my grandson's wife."

Tending the Flock

Jennifer Lagier

They have been waiting nearly their entire lives for this time of day to be fed. As the elderly widow fights upstream through cobwebs and obsolete relics, her old chickens gather and rustle. Carefully, she unhooks the wire door leading from sunlight to the dusty floor of their coop. She lifts each foot like a fragile souffle, remembering last summer's spill and her black and blue hip.

The chickens recognize only her porcelain slop pan. For the first time since she has approached this place of quiet, they nervously croon and discover a common focus for their scattered attention. She begins flinging soggy corners of toast, flaccid carrot stumps and the browning peels from this morning's potatoes. The chickens rush to peck the scattered scraps at her feet.

Varicolored feathers whirl and cackling hens gather around the old woman's ankles. Each has been officially named fifteen years earlier by her youngest son's daughter. Peter Pan, she called the banty. He was the most energetic of all of her roosters. But, when his comb and tail feathers stayed undeveloped, the woman laughed at their mistake and renamed her Pandora. It doesn't matter now, she figures. The granddaughter has discovered boys and no longer visits.

This whole flock is too ancient and decrepit to lay. She knows they wouldn't even be good enough to stew. Besides, she feels rather attached. Pandora there is on her last leg and could go any hour.

Fifteen years. She leans against the gilded apex of a spidery shadow, waiting. Later, she'll edge to her sofa and nap until suppertime happens.

Livvy Caldwell
Barbara Nector Davis

Livvy Caldwell
 sits on all her years
   sometimes they rise on
     beanstalks to her eyes
       scramble to her fingers
         and her toes and then she
           weeps or taps her foot or
             curves her fingers on a melody.
           Livvy sits in a stiff-backed
         chair still as an abandoned
       plow terrified of memories
     forgetting to eat.

Robert Martin Davis, Livvy Caldwell

Translations

Margaret H. Carson

She sits there on the steps and listens
as the wind rustles the dry leaves
of the single maple standing between
the brick apartment building and the street;
but she is hearing wind moving through
pine trees and is once again back
at the lake, lazing an hour away
while children have their midday sleep.
Her foot, pressing against the cement step,
is pushing down upon the forest floor
to make the hammock rock where it is slung
between two trees down by the dock.

She does not see the old car with
the dented fender parked by the curb.
Her white-filmed eyes see only sunlight
glinting on water. The whish of hidden
traffic reaches her as sound of speedboats
racing up the channel.

She lies awake at night and listens to
the shuffling sounds that people in the hallway
make passing her door, and hears again
the scrabbling noises that the bats made
when they came to feed their young, hidden
within the outside double walls.
A wordless shout, down on the street
becomes the half-articulated cry

that sleeping children make, and when a car
sputters in starting out, she hears the snap of twigs
and knows that deer are passing on their way
down to the lake to drink.

Silence that settles both outside and in
is shattered as an ambulance sends out
its chilling cadence in crescendo and diminuendo.
But she is smiling as she falls asleep
hearing the loons' wild, eerie laughter.

To an Old Woman

Rafael Jesús González

Come mother—
    your rebozo trails a black web
    and your hem catches on your heels;
you lean the burden of your years
on shaky cane and palsied hand pushes
    sweat-grimed pennies on the counter.
Can you still see, old woman,
the darting color-trailed needle of your trade?
    The flowers you embroider
    with three-for-a-dime threads
cannot fade as quickly as the leaves of time.
    What things do you remember?
Your mouth seems to be forever tasting
the residue of nectar-hearted years.
    Where are the sons you bore?
Do they speak only English now
and say they're Spanish?
    One day I know you will not come
    and ask for me to pick
    the colors you can no longer see.
I know I'll wait in vain
    for your toothless benediction.
I'll look into the dusty street
made cool by pigeons' wings
until a dirty child will nudge me and say:
    "Señor, how much ees thees?"

The Pianist

Carolyn J. Fairweather Hughes

Gnarled fingers of hands
that were once beautiful
fondle the yellowed keys.

When no one is listening,
she randomly strikes
a few dissonant notes.

Sometimes, I have to turn away
to keep from weeping
at her altered state.

But then, I see
the grey, wrinkled face smile
as chords, precise and graceful,

drop from her hands
like ripened plums.

Occupation
Bonnie Michael Pratt

Women who wait
  in dentists' offices

      while much-loved, freckle-faced children
      go sullenly in to be checked and x-rayed
      and lectured and given rubber toys
      and a new toothbrush to take home.

Women who wait
  in parked cars

      beside dance schools for emotional teenaged
      daughters with acne in scuffed pink ballet shoes
      and tights with runs and leotards
      that are already a size too small.

Women who wait
  in courtrooms

      with hostile lawyers and bored judges
      trying to get more money to pay babysitters
      so they that can go to work and get more money
      to pay attorneys' fees.

Women who wait
  in nursing homes

      to die of uselessness in ivory rooms
      with sterile walls and yellow curtains
      widowed by men who couldn't cry and couldn't touch
      and died of heart attacks.

All the Time

Michael Andrews

It was 93 degrees.
She wore 3 sweaters,
a sweatshirt,
some long pants,
a few dresses,
rolled down nylons,
sneakers,
a feather boa,
and a 47 year old mink.
She bought the mink
for consolation
the day she outlived
her last husband.
One eyelid
was in a flutter
of perpetual motion.
Lipstick
ran all over her face
like a map of Chicago.
She was as crazy
as a 5 oclock commuter.
Went to the Safeway
twice a week
with molding dollars,
social security checks,
and food stamps.
Stole Tootsie Rolls
and ate them before

she left the market.
Walked to the intersection.
Waited for the light
to turn red,
hunched low,
knees high,
lurched out in front
of oncoming traffic,
waved madly at
the skidding cars,
her wire basket
with coffee, doughnuts
and smoked oysters
bouncing right behind her,
chuckling and muttering
about insane drivers,
one eyeball rotating
in an orgasm of fear.

It was her little joke.

Once a policeman stopped her.
She kicked him in the shin,
scattered his citations
all over the street,
yelled rape
in her reed-pipe voice
and scurried home
muttering about cops.
After that
the police left her alone,
but sometimes they
spoiled the fun
by stopping the traffic
at her favorite crosswalk.

Her house buzzed
with ticking clocks.
She didn't trust the electric ones.
Wound all 217 of them every day,
but never set the time.
She considered the random
firing of alarms
a form of music.
She kept the smoked oysters
for the dog in the freezer
with her third husband's appendix,
which the dog greatly desired.
But the old lady kept it
in memory of the surgeon
she married after he performed
the appendectomy in which
her third husband died
of cancer of everything.
Sometimes at night
she beat on the windows
across the airshaft
with a broom handle,
shouted obscenities and yelled
"You keep quiet in there.
You keep quiet."

After a while
they sealed up the windows.
It was getting harder
all the time
to get someone's
attention.

Bag Ladies in L.A.

Savina A. Roxas

Sunday on Santa Monica Boulevard
people stiffen and turn away
like Calder mobiles
when bag ladies kneel
to mark territorial
imperatives in vacant doorways
with the L.A. TIMES
from trash cans, brush
their teeth with water
from discarded Smucker's
jars, and defecate at the curb,
— Rest Rooms Closed on Sunday —
bundle into a corner
with eyes that stalk those who
walk the palatial Boulevard
neither santa nor monica.

Photo by Rod Bradley

glory
Charlotte Watson Sherman

honey, i just sit here mindin my own business. i just act like i'm a part of this old stone building. i like to watch people try not to look at me. like they're scared they might end up here too. but you know, it ain't always that bad. specially in the summer. i likes to sit here and watch folks. the other day i saw a man with a miniskirt on. lord have mercy. he sure looked a mess. and he had purple hair. the color of the church robes over at macedonia blood on the cross a.m.e. oh, i know it ain't nothin like the old a.m.e church that used to plot about colored folks freedom. but i went anyway. well, people just too much into stylin and profilin for my taste. and i wasn't scared to stand up and tell the preacher that to his face. maybe i shouldn't have done it in the middle of his sermon. but, he wasn't like no preacher we had back home, that's for sure. with his mouth all pinched up, trying to talk like some old white man. i sure did tell him. i said rev, why dontcha put some fire in your words & make us feel somethin. anything. i like to feel like i'm likkered up when i hear a good sermon. but this man wasn't even close to heatin up old sarah philips. and she can get happy over just about anything. and even she was sittin there lookin like a pew. but i don't go back there no more. and i guess they glad. i don't like nobody escortin a grown woman nowhere. especially out of no church in front of them old pretend-to-be-christian people. honey, i know them folks. i see plenty of em walkin down this very street. and they don't even turn they heads. now that's a christian for you. can't wait to get to church on sunday to moan about jesus and if he was right here on earth starin em in the face, they'd probably spit on him and keep on walking. just like they do me. now, i can get along pretty good with most of these winos down here. they don't mess with me too much. they know i ain't got no quarter to give em to buy a bottle and i cuss em out good and loud when they forget and try to panhandle me. now, i know they'll try to take advantage of some of the women down here that go around lookin like stray rabbits. and i done told a few of em to get em a piece of broken whiskey bottle and keep it right next to em so when some fool tries to get funny and starts rubbin up on em or grabbin on em they can either pull the piece out and give em a warning or they can do what i had to do one time and don't give no warning, just stick em. that'll teach em to leave you alone. see, they thinks i'm crazy. and ain't nothin a wino scared of more than a crazy woman down here. cept for not havin no more wine in life, of course. honey, sometimes i'll rise up like a tornado and just start spoutin scripture, right and left. and i'll walk up and down the street and maybe stand on the corner for a while and flag down cars. that's just to remind these folks that i'm still alive and not a stone wall. i just look this way. but i got a heap of sense. you know i never thought i'd be able to pack up all my life and put it in a paper bag. all my life in a paper bag. but it ain't so bad sometimes. i'm portable and i can go anywhere. i'm just tired of moving on. and i can wash up every day right here in the jailhouse bathroom. and i do keep myself clean. you know god takes care of fools and babies. i take care of myself. so it ain't so bad. really. i just sit and try to blend into the walls.

Old Women
Barbara Lau

Old women
wrap scarves around their necks
to hide their wrinkles,
and flatter their bosoms
with bold beads and brooches.
In dresses buttered with flowers,
in voices light as Baby's Breath,
how they bloom in the corner
of the cafeteria, billowing
over pictures of grandchildren
passed round and round like hors d'oeuvres
like jewels they plant on each hand
to occupy the spaces once held
and warmed by husbands.

Now twined around each other
arm in arm down the sidewalk,
defying the dark grave
with their colors and perfume,
old women
tending time more fragile than youth:
poinsettias in the snow.

Bag Ladies

Ruth Harriet Jacobs

We are all bag ladies
or becoming so.
Nothing lasts
not love
or the beloved
or hope
even mountains crumble
only the ocean waits
to catch our tears

Bags of memories
tell us who we were
before we were wise

The bags burden us.
Carrying about
our losses,
we stumble
clutching our unfreedom
against all threats
or promises
it being all we have
it being all we know
it being all we are.

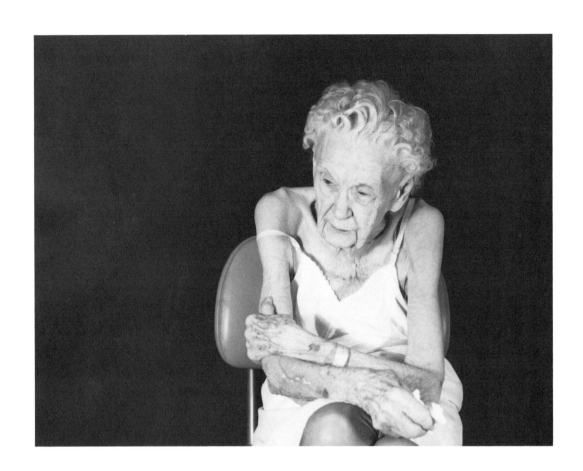

Endings
Lynn Kozma

Frail as porcelain
she sits, unmoving
except for bone-thin hands
mending with care
forgotten clothes
which are not there —
threading unseen needles,
moistening fingertips
from parchment lips,
knotting the thread
carefully.

There — one more finished —
smoothing the wrinkles away,
softly laying it by,
slipping back
to the early May
of her life
as easily as breathing.

My planet — earth;
hers — a distant star.
Impossible to travel
that far.

Lori Burkhalter, Grace

Last Visit to Grandmother

Enid Shomer

I enter through a forest
of crystal stemware,
down a Persian runner path.
Bedridden, but still elegant,
her hair a bluish wisp of August sky,
she sits up to eat, seems
to watch TV, but cannot speak.

The objects she mothered
tend her now: gilt sconces,
cranberry lustres,
the japanned dresser
where hinged family photographs
cluster like butterflies.

She grabs my hand and pats it,
giggling like an infant
who has just discovered its toes.
Then she winces, covers her mouth,
points to her dentures,
brushes a crumb from the sheets.

Her nurse interrupts to take her
to the bathroom. The patient's
body, she points out, is spotless
as her Grand Baroque: all those
intricate folds of skin
and not one bedsore.

When I leave, the nurse
is helping her change for evening.
A small virtue to want to die
as she lived: in a good
silk dress, some detail
like bugle beads
at the collar and cuffs.

Words for Alice after Her Death

Angela Peckenpaugh

It came by surprise
like a blown fuse,
an old car you were used to
for a few errands, stolen.
We made room in our busy lives
to deal with your loss
as we had your illness.
You asked so little
I'm stumped with your elegy.
I'd rather rub your back
at your request,
or deal a hand of gin rummy.
At your own death you might
have let out one of your
high pitched sighs, your
reaction when landing on a chair,
shock of contact,
relief at getting there.

Now your old blue robe,
as familiar as the dark
green kitchen walls
will be in the last load
of laundry. The Fanny Farmer
box that held the savored
chocolate candy will
be emptied in the trash,
another act done

by one or two people
who kept looking in.

There won't be too much to move,
contents of closet, bureau, desk,
a bed and a few old chairs.
We already went through the pantry,
the spare room, eliminating
all but the nostalgic and necessary.

I find myself seeing your smile,
so welcome. It told of pain
for the time forgotten
in the pleasure of my brief company.
You were so grateful
for small acts of kindness
it was easy to feel blessed
for manicure, bed change,
buying a shower cap at the 5 & 10.
I see your white hair, eyes peeking
over the front door glass,
a blown kiss to assure me
you were safe inside,
but, frail package, how could
you be, really. That was
the old nurse's trick, to grin
and bear it, inquire about my health
first thing by phone call
in the morning. Yes,
you remembered my latest worry
and gave it an airing, before
we decided when I would see you.
I forgive you your resistances

to my consoling schemes —
for turning down good mystery books
because your eyes were failing,
for wearing the dress from India
only once, because the sleeves were tight,
and for picking at a Chinese dish
in a restaurant I had chosen.

Now I regret how little
your coin collection added up to
when I took it to the gold exchange.
The clerk said sometimes customers
salted the kitty for grandmothers
because they couldn't believe
how little their life savings
had come to. How little it all
comes to. But I used to remind you
at least you had interesting friends —
Buddhists and poets, an actor or two
and you agreed. And left alone
stains of fear and disease
on the sheets but didn't stain
our consciences with demands
we couldn't answer.
"What is the name of those beans?"
you wanted to know, embarrassed
to have forgotten.
I think I said every kind — pinto, string,
lima, green. But it was an avocado
that Jeff brought you,
on your mind. Hard to grasp,
like your bravery at the end,
trips down the old steps

to the washing machine,
outings in the car
to our affairs, picnic, rummage sale,
art show, when for you
a slow walk from bed to front room
must have seemed a trip to the moon.
It was no small feat
to heat up hamburger and add frozen
potatoes to the grease,
creating a little Yorkshire pudding,
that left you pleased.
Your presence now is like the backrub
you tried to give me—the touch is
weak but gentle, and full of apology.

The Thugs
Mura Dehn

The years don't serve their time,
they're runaways,
they bump each other off
sun up, sun down.

Time, master mugger,
snatched this century
out of my hands
and fled.

The Coming of Winter
Shirley Vogler Meister

The winter winds have chilled the warmth we knew
and whirl our unmet dreams like crumbling leaves
around the barren trees: a rendezvous
of weathered bones and somber dance which weaves
despair with sparks of hope that summon spring.
Beyond the wailing wind is sanguine sound —
the vigor-voice that wakes all slumbering —
the reassuring call of power more profound.

We acquiesce to freezing winds and test
our mettle 'gainst the spectral storms ahead,
for there are forces that we can't arrest
and states of nature that we need not dread.
Beyond the winds lie gentler joys and peace
that sanctify our fate and death's caprice.

Post Humus
Patti Tana

Scatter my ashes in my garden
so I can be near my loves.
Say a few honest words, sing a gentle song,
join hands in a circle of flesh.
Please tell some stories about me
making you laugh. I love to make you laugh.
When I've had time to settle, and green
gathers into buds, remember I love blossoms
bursting in spring. As the season ripens
remember my persistent passion.
And if you come in my garden
on an August afternoon
pluck a bright red globe,
let juice run down your chin and the seeds
stick to your cheek.   When I'm dead
I want folks to smile and say   *That Patti,*
she sure is some tomato!

Lori Burkhalter, Untitled

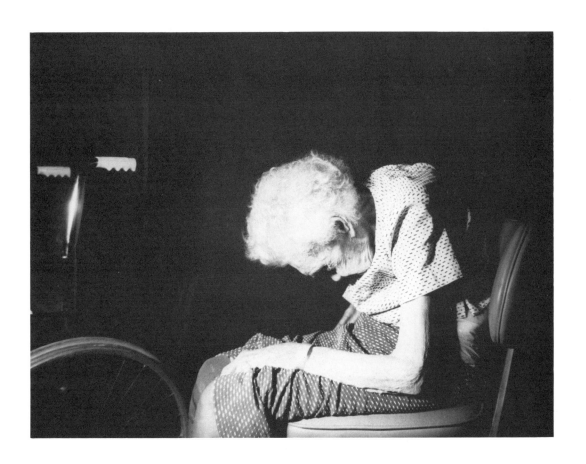

Life's Rainbow

Sheila Banani

Beginnings are lacquer red
    fired hard in the kiln
    of hot hope;

Middles, copper yellow
    in sunshine,
    sometimes oxidize green
    with tears; but

Endings are always indigo
    before we step
    on the other shore.

John Renner, Bubba

About the Contributors:

MICHAEL ANDREWS is a southern California publisher, editor, and printer for Bombshelter Press. His books include *Poems for Amber, 3 Begats, Xmas Tree Massacre, 40 Turkeys So What, A Telegram Unsigned, Gnomes and the Xmas Kid,* and three fine print books/portfolios of poetry and photography: *Riverrun, Machu Picchu,* and *Riding South.*

DORI APPEL, a poet, playwright, and fiction writer, is also an actress and co-Director of Mixed Company Theatre in Ashland, OR. Her play "Female Troubles," co-authored with Carolyn Myers, has toured nationally. "Birthday Portrait in Muted Tones" was awarded 2nd place in the "Poet's Choice" contest sponsored by the Oregon State Poetry Association in 1986.

MARY ANNE ASHLEY, a resident of northern California, studied poetry writing with Kate Rennie Archer at the Dominican Upper School in San Rafael. Her stories have appeared in *Quindaro 15* and *Quindaro 16* and were read on public radio. She belongs to the Virginia Woolf Society and the International Geranium Society and would join the Rote Zora if she just knew how.

SHEILA BANANI from Santa Monica, CA, earned her BA and MA from UCLA. A former sociology instructor and coastal planner, her poetry has been published in *World Order Quarterly, The Peace Maker,* and *Abiding Silence, An Anthology.*

SARAH BARNHILL lives and writes in the mountains of western North Carolina where she also teaches at a small college and is a student in the MFA program at Warren Wilson College. Her fiction and nonfiction have appeared in numerous magazines, including *Appalachian Heritage, Cold Mountain Review,* and *Summit.*

THERESE BECKER is a member of the National Press Photographer's Association. Her work has appeared in the major Detroit newspapers, *Heritage Magazine, Metropolitan Detroit Magazine,* and other publications.

TOM BENEDIKTSSON lives and teaches in northern New Jersey. He is the author of a critical book on the San Francisco poet George Sterling, and of a growing number of published and unpublished poems.

ELIZABETH BENNETT received her BA Cum Laude from Bryn Mawr College and has pursued graduate studies at George Mason University. She was the 1987 winner of the Irene Leache Memorial Award for free verse. Her poems have appeared in *Phoebe, Poet Lore,* and *The New York Times.* She is presently living, writing, and aging in McLean, VA.

BARBARA BOLZ lives in Kansas City with her husband, Tim Houghton, with whom she co-edits *Panoply,* a new magazine of poetry. Her work has been published in many magazines, including *Colorado-North Review, Negative Capability,* and *The Bloomsbury Review.*

CATHERINE BOYD, a resident of Santa Rosa, CA, has had short stories published in *Ridge Review* and *The Stump.* Several of her feature articles have appeared in the

Marin/Sonoma section of the *San Francisco Examiner,* one of the city's leading newspapers.

ROD BRADLEY is a novelist and photographer living in Los Angeles. His photographs have been exhibited with William Eggleston and Ansel Adams.

KAREN BRODINE, a Seattle based teacher, typesetter and book designer, has been published widely in the feminist, lesbian/gay, and left press. She has had four books of poetry published, including *Workweek* and *Illegal Assembly,* and recently edited and designed *Socialist Feminism: The First Decade* by Gloria Martin.

LORI BURKHALTER currently lives and works as a photographer in Los Angeles. She is a graduate of the Otis Parsons Art Institute.

GRACE BUTCHER's work has been appearing in little magazines since the 60s; her most recent books are *Rumors of Ecstasy...Rumors of Death* and *Before I Go Out on the Road.* An associate professor of English at Kent State, OH, Ms. Butcher is a three-time US half-mile champion who won the 400/800m in the 50-54 age group at the 1984 Masters Pan American Games, and, at the 1985 World Games in Rome, took a 4th and 5th in the 1500/800m.

BILLIE LOU CANTWELL teaches creative writing workshops and writes from her home in east Texas. Her poetry, articles, short stories, and novels have appeared in such publications as *Worchester Review, Byline,* and *Descant.*

MARGARET H. CARSON, a nurse until her retirement, began writing poetry in her late fifties. Since then a number of her poems have appeared in *Festival,* a publication sponsored by the Friends of the Steele Memorial Library in Elmira, NY, where she resides.

ELLIN CARTER, a Columbus, OH, writer, teacher and feminist, came to poetry late (in her mid-forties) and began writing in earnest and submitting her work for publication in 1975. Her work has appeared in *Negative Capability, Anima, Women's Quarterly Review,* and other magazines and anthologies.

LYN COWAN began photographing seriously five years ago. She has had four exhibitions and has had numerous photographs published in magazines, journals, and local Minneapolis newspapers. Making pictures of older women began in 1985 with the "Whisper, Minnesota" project and continues as a personal interest. In her other life she is a Jungian analyst.

BARBARA NECTOR DAVIS is an editor, poet, and novelist whose work has been published in numerous journals and anthologies. *The Journey and Elders of the Tribe* is a collection of her poetry, illustrated by her photographer husband, Robert Martin Davis. In 1986 she was awarded first place in the Family of God International Poetry Competition. She and Robert live in Marietta, GA.

ROBERT MARTIN DAVIS has been engaged in photography virtually all of his life. In 1984, after a successful one man show, he retired from his position as Senior Administrative Law Judge to devote all his time to photography. He has won numerous awards and is a member of the Cobb Photographic Society, Marietta Fine Arts Center and the South Cobb Arts Alliance, which hosted his most recent one man show.

MURA DEHN was a Russian-born dancer, choreographer, and film maker who became known as a specialist in American black dance. A pioneer in documenting the various styles of black social dance, she directed a company of black dancers until 1973. She started writing poetry when she was in her seventies. Ms. Dehn died unexpectedly in her home in New York City in February, 1987, at the age of 84.

SUE SANIEL ELKIND began writing at the age of 64 with no formal training. She has had over 300 poems published in over 100 magazines. Her first book, *No Longer Afraid,* was published in 1985 and her second book, *Waiting for Order,* is forthcoming. She founded and runs the Squirrel Hill Poetry Workshop sponsored by the Carnegie Library in Pittsburgh, PA.

RINA FERRARELLI, a Pittsburgh teacher, writer, and translator of poetry, graduated from Carlow College and Duquesne University. Her work has appeared in several publications, including *The Dream Book: An Anthology of Writings by Italian-American Women* (Selocken Books), *The Hudson Review, Literary Review, Poetry Now* and *Tar River Poetry.* Her first collection of translations, *Light Without Motion,* is forthcoming from Owl Creek Press.

MARGARET FLANAGAN EICHER, a resident of upstate New York, has had poems published in various magazines and anthologies, including *The Haven, Alternative Fiction and Poetry,* and *On The Line.* In its first issue, *The Caribbean Writer* published one of her earlier poems, written in 1948 when she was still in the Women's Army Corps in the Panama Canal Zone.

CAROLE L. GLICKFELD, a resident of Seattle, was born and raised in New York City, the setting of *Useful Gifts,* a recently completed collection of childhood stories. Other poems and stories have appeared in *South Coast Poetry Journal* and *The Gamut,* and her play, *The Challenge,* has been performed by numerous elderly groups around the country.

RAFAEL JESÚS GONZÁLEZ, a Berkeley, CA, teacher and writer, received his education at the University of Texas at El Paso, Universidad Nacional Autónoma de México, and the University of Oregon. Widely published in reviews and anthologies in the US, Mexico, and abroad, his collection of verse, *El Hacedor de Huegos/The Maker of Games,* went into a second printing.

EDNA J. GUTTAG's poetry, short stories, and articles have appeared in such publications as *The New York Times* and *News World.* A resident of New York City, she recieved the Joyce Kilmer Award from NYU. She is a member of a literary discussion group and a supporter of both the theatre and the opera.

DAME HYACINTHE HILL, a resident of Putnam Valley, NY, is a poet, painter, editor, and educator. The author of *Shoots of a Vagrant Vine* (Avalon National Book Award), *Promethea, Squaw No More,* and *Poetry and the Stars,* her poetry has received many awards and has been internationally translated and published. She was named International Poet Laureate for 1973, 1974, and 1975.

CAROLYN J. FAIRWEATHER HUGHES writes for a newspaper and magazine in Pittsburgh, PA. Her poems have appeared in many literary magazines, including *Sage Woman, Kindred Spirits,* and *Yet Another Small Magazine.*

RUTH HARRIET JACOBS, PhD, is a Wellesley, MA, sociologist, gerontologist, playwright, poet, and activist on behalf of women, older people, and peace. She is the author of four books, including *Life After Youth: Female, Forty, What Next?, Button, Button, Who Has the Button?,* and *Older Women Surviving and Thriving.* Dr. Jacobs is the founding mother of Responsible Aging Smart People (RASP).

SUSAN S. JACOBSON has worked in journalism, public relations, prison reform, sports, mental health, and higher education. Her poetry has appeared in *Pudding 10, Poetic Moods Quarterly 1984,* and *Further Prayers from the Ark* and her work has been read in poetry therapy for the past several years. She attended college at Bryn Mawr and Elmira and lives in Washington, PA.

TERRI L. JEWELL is a 32 year old black lesbian feminist from Lansing, MI. She won the "New Voices" poetry contest in 1986 and her work has appeared in over 200 small press publications, including *Conditions, Sing Heavenly Muse,* and *Black American Literature Forum.*

JENNY JOSEPH, a poet and writer from Gloucestershire, England, has published four volumes of poetry and six children's books. Her latest book of prose and verse, *Persephone,* won the James Tait Memorial Book Prize for fiction in 1986.

SUSAN A. KATZ, a resident of New York, is the author of two poetry collections: *Two Halves of the Same Silence* and *The Separate Sides of Need.* Her poems have appeared in numerous magazines, including *Kansas Quarterly, The Smith,* and *Bitterroot.*

RICK KEMPA is a tutor for the Writing Skills Improvement Program in Tucson, AZ, and has an MFA from the University of Arizona. "Grandma Sits Down" is set in the ranch-lands of southern Idaho, and honors Fern Callen, "one of the most special people in my world."

LYNN KOZMA, a resident of West Islip, NY, is a retired registered nurse who served in the Army Nurse Corps, Air Forces, in World War II. She started writing seriously six years ago and has been published in *Bitterroot, The Lyric,* and *The Country Poet.* Her poetry has won several awards, including *Midwest Poetry Review's* 1985 honored poem of the year.

MARISA LABOZZETTA is a graduate of Boston College and Georgetown University Graduate School of Language and Linguistics. Her fiction has appeared in *Pandora, The Florida Review,* and *The American Voice.* In 1980 she won first prize in short fiction in The Rio Grande Writers' Literary Competition.

JENNIFER LAGIER is a librarian/storyteller from the Central Valley of California who now lives in Monterey. Her work has appeared in a variety of publications, including *Touchstone, Women's Compendium,* and *Crazy Quilt.* She graduated from California State University, Stanislaus, and UC Berkeley and is Co-area Coordinator for the California Poets in the Schools.

BARBARA LAU, a Texan living in Decatur, IL, has published numerous feature articles in national publications such as *Working Woman, Savvy,* and *Family Circle,* but poetry and fiction are her first love. Her work will be featured this year in the Sangamon State University literary magazine: *The Alchemist.* In 1986 she won 2nd place in the

Christopher Morley Memoriam Poetry Contest at the University of Texas at Austin.

DORIS VANDERLIPP MANLEY has been writing poetry almost continuously since her high school days when she won a competition for a collection of verse which, "fortuitously, has long since perished along with the lurid magenta silk cover I laboriously made for it." A resident of Cherry Valley, NY, she has had several poems recently selected for anthologies.

SHIRLEY VOGLER MEISTER, an Indianapolis free-lance writer, has had over 150 poems and light verses—as well as reviews, articles, and essays—accepted by diverse publications throughout the US. She earned a belated BA in English (with highest distinction) in 1985 from Indiana University. Recognition for her writing includes Purdue University Literary Awards for poetry, literary criticism, and journalism.

S. MINANEL, while in her twenties, became the first woman editor in comic books, writing one-page fillers, games and puzzles for *Archie Comics*. After moving to California, she began doing doggerel and nautical-type graphics, which have appeared in *Personal Computer Age, AB Bookman's Weekly, Sailing Magazine* and *Pacific Yachting,* amongst others.

JANICE TOWNLEY MOORE is a native of Atlanta who teaches in the English Department at Young Harris College in the north Georgia mountains. Her poems have appeared in numerous publications such as *Southern Poetry Review, Florida Review,* and *New Virginia Review.* She is poetry editor of *Georgia Journal.*

LILLIAN MORRISON, a resident of New York City, is the author of thirteen books: six collections of her own poetry (most recently *The Break Dance Kids*), six collection of folk rhymes for children, and one anthology of sports poetry. Her poems have appeared in numerous publications such as *Atlantic Monthly, Images,* and *Light Year.* A new anthology, *Rhythm Road; Poems to Move to,* is forthcoming. She received the Grolier Award at the 1987 American Library Association Conference.

MICHELLE NOULLET is a teacher and poet who has been working in the Southeast Asian refugee camps since 1980. She lives "in the last town on the road before you fall into the South China Sea."

ANGELA PECKENPAUGH teaches at the University of Wisconsin at Whitewater. She is the author of *Letters from Lee's Army, Discovering the Mandala* and *A Book of Charms.* Her work has been published in numerous publications including *Greenfield Review, Abraxas* and *Small Press Review. Refreshing the Fey,* a group of fairy tale based poems, was recently published by Sackbut Press.

FIONNA PERKINS, a reporter, feature writer, and editor for the *San Francisco News,* became involved in political campaigning and feminist writing in the late 50s and completed her first novel in the 60s. Her work has appeared in publications such as *Fiction West, Stories, Ridge Review* and *The Land of Six Seasons.* She lives on the coast of northern California.

FRAN PORTLEY majored in English Honors at Duke University for two years. She lives in northern New Jersey where she has taught poetry to children and led poetry workshops for adults. Her poems have appeared in publications such as *Stone Country,*

Heartland and *The Charlotte Observer.*

BONNIE MICHAEL PRATT is a freelance writer and poet living in Winston-Salem, NC, whose special interest is women's issues. Her poetry has received numerous awards and has been published in *The Lyricist, The Arts Journal, Appalachian Heritage, The Colonnades,* two anthologies and commercial magazines.

SANDRA REDDING is a grandmother and student in the MFA writing program at the University of North Carolina at Greensboro. Her work has appeared in several regional journals, including *The Crucible, Village Writer* and *Share.* Five of her short stories have been published in anthologies.

JOHN RENNER is a psychiatric social worker who counsels high school students with learning disabilities. He uses photography as one way of building relationships with students. John's photographs often appear with Patti Tana's poetry. "Bubba" is a picture of their son Jesse and Jesse's grandmother Ada ("Bubba").

ELISAVIETTA RITCHIE, a Washington, DC, writer, poet, translator, teacher, and editor, has published several prize winning collections of poetry and short stories. Her work has appeared in numerous publications, including *The Christian Science Monitor, The New York Times* and *The Washington Post.* Having received a BA degree from the University of California in Berkeley and a master's degree from the American University, she is the founder of *The Wineberry Press* and is editing an anthology of poems on endangered marine species: *Tide Turning.*

MARIE KENNEDY ROBINS, taken kicking and screaming from the South at age five, returned after fifty years of urban gridlock. She began to write short stories and poems after she burned out as a teacher and has been published in several states. She records for public radio with a group called Writers Ink in Fayetteville, NC. Her work won first prize in a contest sponsored by the North Carolina Poetry Society.

SAVINA A. ROXAS, a freelance writer from Pittsburgh, holds a PhD in Library and Information Sciences and is a former professor with Clarion State University. Her poetry and short stories have appeared in many publications such as *Black Fly Review, Wind Chimes* and *Night Times.*

VICTORIA THERESA SALLOUM earned a BA degree in Journalism from Loyola University in New Orleans, LA, where she resides. In 1976 her feature writing for *The Palm Beach Daily News* in Palm Beach, FL, won an award from the Florida Society of Newspaper Editors.

DEIDRE SCHERER is a Williamsville, VT, artist who "paints" with fabric and thread, using unusual cutting, layering and machine stitching techniques to achieve illusionistic effects. Her portraits of the elderly have traveled in solo and in collaborative exhibitions. Ms. Scherer holds a fine arts degree from the Rhode Island School of Design.

BETTIE SELLERS, Goolsby Professor of English at Young Harris College in northern Georgia, has published five collections of poems, the latest being *Liza's Monday and Other Poems.* Her poems have appeared in such journals as the *The Georgia Review, Poem* and *The Appalachian Heritage.* Ms. Sellers received the 1987 Governor's Award in the Humanities for exemplary achievement in fostering an understanding and appreciation of the humanities in Georgia.

JOANNE SELTZER, an upstate New York writer and poet, has published several short stories, a chapbook, *Adirondack Lake Poems,* and a number of literary essays. Over 200 of her poems have appeared in a wide variety of literary journals, anthologies and classroom texts.

CHARLOTTE WATSON SHERMAN, a resident of Seattle, has had poetry published in *The Black Scholar, Obsidian* and *Gathering Ground: New Writing and Art by Northwest Women of Color.* Forthcoming work includes *Nia and the Golden Stool* and *Shattered Glass: Violence in the Lives of Black Women.* Her choreo-poem, "Erzulie," will be produced by The Women's Theatre.

ENID SHOMER's poems appear in *Poetry, The Women's Review of Books, Helicon Nine, Coda,* and other magazines and anthologies. In 1985-86 she received an Individual Artist's Grant in Poetry from the State of Florida. She is the author of *Stalking the Florida Panther* (1987), winner of the booklength competition of The Word Works, as well as two chapbooks: *The Startle Effect* (1983) and *Florida Postcards* (1987), winner of the 1986 Jubilee Press Chapbook Competition.

PATTI TANA teaches at Nassau Community College, SUNY, and is on the editorial board of *Esprit: A Humanities Magazine.* She participated in the production and performance of an album of women's work songs, *The Work of the Women,* and is author of two books of poetry: *How Odd This Ritual of Harmony* and *Ask the Dreamer Where the Night Begins.*

RANDEANE TETU has received three national awards for fiction. A resident of Haddam, CT, her work has been published in *The Massachusetts Review, Loonfeather* and *New England Sampler.* She has written two collections of short stories and is currently working on her second novel.

CINDA THOMPSON is a graduate of Southern Illinois University and the University of Arizona in Tucson. A former teacher, she now works as a production editor in Peoria, IL. She has been published in *Iowa Woman* and *Embers Magazine* and won 3rd place in the 1983 Virginia Highlands Festival Contest (short fiction) and in the 1984 National Poetry Collective Contest.

JESS WELLS is a San Francisco Bay area lesbian whose fifth book, *The Dress/The Sharda Stories,* is available from Library B Books. Her new collection of short stories, *Two Willow Chairs,* is forthcoming.

MICHELE WOLF, a magazine editor from New York City, has had poetry published in *Confrontation, The Greenfield Review, Cottonwood Review* and other literary journals. Her awards include a Literature Career Award from the National Society of Arts and Letters, a Bread Loaf Writer's Conference scholarship, and residency fellowships from the Virginia Center for the Creative Arts and the Helene Wurlitzer Foundations in Taos, NM.

MARCIA WOODRUFF earned her BA in English from Smith College, her MAT from Harvard University and, after a twenty-five year interval, a PhD from the University of Louisville. Her poetry and fiction have appeared in the *American Voice* and *Louisville Review.* In 1986 she was the recipient of a writing grant from the Kentucky Foundation for Women.

Papier-Maché Press Distribution Services

Additional copies of *When I Am an Old Woman I Shall Wear Purple* are available through your local bookstore or from Papier-Maché Press for $10.00 plus postage and handling. We are also pleased to offer the following:

T-shirts, *When I Am an Old Woman I Shall Wear Purple,* choice of purple or white, regular cut, S, M, L, XL, $10.00

A special offering of note cards featuring the fabric and thread "paintings" of Deidre Scherer:

> Group I – A packet of six note cards including three each of "Freida" and "Laughing Rose," the cover art from *When I Am an Old Woman I Shall Wear Purple,* $5.70.

> Group II – A special collection of three note cards accompanied by hospice messages on separate inserts, includes one each of "Jade Dream," "Under Twilight," and "Reaching Leaves," $4.50.

Atalanta, an anthology of creative work celebrating women's athletic achievements, 54 pages of poetry, prose and photography, Papier-Maché, $4.00. "A collection of tales that describe the softer side, the underside, the fluidity, the grace. If you've never quite been able to explain desire, determination or defeat to your non-athletic friends, consider giving them this book." Mariah Burton Nelson, *Women's Sports and Fitness Magazine.*

More Golden Apples, a further celebration of women and sport, 56 page collection of poetry and prose, Papier-Maché, $5.95. "...A strong, distinctive voice able to distill the author's experience, as well as provide a mirror in which we can see more of ourselves." Audrey Ferber, *Women's Sports and Fitness Magazine.*

Other Selections from Our Distinguished Contributors:

Ask the dreamer where night begins, by Patti Tana, a collection of 61 poems, 21 essays, and numerous writing suggestions, Kendall/Hunt Publishing Company, $11.95. The story of a girl growing into womanhood, told in a natural voice – resonant and accessible. "...A concerto in words, complete with coda. Here is music that will haunt the reader's mind." Dr. Alfred Dorn, former Vice-President of the Poetry Society of America.

Refreshing the Fey, by Angela Peckenpaugh, a chapbook of eleven poems, Sackbut Press, $3.00. Based on Celtic lore and fairly tales, this collection contains both wisdom and humor.

A Book of Charms, by Lois Beebe and Angela Peckenpaugh, a book of spells, Barnwood Press, $5.00.

Discovering the Mandala, by Angela Peckenpaugh, a collection of poems, Lakes and Prairies Press, $3.00. Poetry on a Jungian theme.

Rumors of Ecstasy...Rumors of Death, by Grace Butcher, 38 poems, Barnwood Press, $5.00. Currently in its third printing, this collection has found a wide audience. "Lucid, original work, accessible through its simplicity. She writes mostly on the major themes – love and death – sometimes with a strange whimsy." Bobbie Goodwin, former editor, *Bachy* magazine.

Before I Go Out On the Road, by Grace Butcher, 34 poems, Cleveland State University Poetry Center, $5.00. Poetry from the heart chronicling Ms. Butcher's physical and emotional journeys. "The writer as runner, as motorcyclist, as poet. She has a clear voice that does not depend on flashy tricks but communicates in straightforward language her unique perceptions." Bobbie Goodwin, former editor, *Bachy* magazine.

Reaching into Our Heads Stealing Buckets of Flame, by Jennifer Lagier, a chapbook of 16 poems, $2.00. "With vivid imagery and striking use of metaphor she transforms even simple, growing fruit into something new, important, ominous. Her strong voice is applied here to living, loving, dreams – the real stuff." Elizabeth Grey, Director, Westside Writer's Group.

Raking the Snow, by Elisavietta Ritchie, poetry, 54 pages, $4.00. Selected by the Washington Writer's Publishing House in their 1982 poetry competition. "Grim, joyous, exuberant, or erotic, they have a strong and vivid life." Josephine Jacobson, former poetry consultant, Library of Congress.

Tightening the Circle Over Eel Country, by Elisavietta Ritchie, poetry, 112 pages, collector's item, includes author's corrections, $3.75. Awarded the Great Lakes Colleges Association "New Writer's Award for Best First Book of Poetry, 1975-76." "Combines a Byzantine elegance with straightforward, plain style honesty. The extraordinary range of her interests...is reinforced by her exquisite regard for language and a lively fascination with the possibility of form." William Packard, Editor of *New York Quarterly.*

The Problem with Eden, by Elisavietta Ritchie, 24 pages, $2.50. Winner of the 1985 Poetry Society of Georgia's Armstrong State College Press Chapbook Competition. "The choice was difficult but ultimately her assurance, wide range of tones and voices, and consistently high quality won." Competition Judge.

Writing Home, a collection of poems by Katharyn Machan Aal and Barbara Crooker, 35 poems, Gehry Press, $4.50. "Katharyn Aal sees and shares the subtleties and intricacies that reveal the inner nature of relationships — with friend, dying mentor, lover, and fellow poet. Her words glide and are beautiful, even when they convey sadness.

Barbara Crooker uses nature as metaphor. Through growing things and changing seasons, she speaks of hearts that migrate, hope that beauty will reappear, faith that makes us plant gardens. In the cycle of sprouting, growing, ripening, and harvest, nature and spirit connect with a satisfying sense of wholeness." Elizabeth Grey, Director, Westside Writer's Group.

The Dress/The Sharda Stories, by Jess Wells, 126 page collection of short stories, $7.95. "Jess Wells writes with exuberant energy and style. Whether trying on an outrageously femme dress in a thrift store or journeying through our collective past, her dyke characters move with honesty and dash...Read this book, for fun, for excitement, for good writing. You won't be disappointed." Sandy Boucher, author of *Heartwomen.*

Two Willow Chairs, by Jess Wells, 126 pages, $8.95. Beautifully crafted short stories of lesbian lives and loves, this new book is rich, subtle and complex. "I read *Two Willow Chairs* and wept and was glad. How nice at last to have sentiment about our lives, our deaths..." Kate Millett, author of *Sexual Politics.*

Older Women: Surviving and Thriving, by Dr. Ruth Harriet Jacobs, Family Service America, $17.95. A self-help manual outlining a 12-session group workshop designed to help older women deal with stereotypes, employment, loneliness, sexuality, health maintenance, finances, and living arrangements. "A lot of people become patronizing and talk about pathology when they think of older women. Dr. Jacobs is at the forefront of honoring their wisdom and their skills." Marjorie Glassman, Director of services for older people at Family Service of Greater Boston.

Please add $1.00 for the first item and $.50 for each additional item to cover postage and handling. Mail check or money order for the full amount with your name and address to:

Papier-Maché Press
795 Via Manzana
Watsonville, CA 95076
(408) 726-2933